God,
the Father of Mercy

To Lynn
From Award
Christmas 98
Peace

God,
the Father of Mercy

Prepared by
The Theological-Historical Commission
for the Great Jubilee of the Year 2000

Translated from the Italian by
Robert R. Barr

A Herder and Herder Book
The Crossroad Publishing Company
New York

The Crossroad Publishing Company
370 Lexington Avenue, New York, NY 10017

Original edition: *Dio, Padre di misericordia*
Copyright © 1998 by Edizioni San Paolo (Milan)

English translation Copyright © 1998 by
The Crossroad Publishing Company

Printed in the United States of America

Library of Congress Cataloging-in-Publication Data
Dio, padre di misericordia. English.
    God, the father of mercy / prepared by the Theological-Historical
Commission for the Great Jubilee of the Year 2000 ; translated from
the Italian by Robert R. Barr.
        p.   cm.
    "A Herder & Herder book."
    ISBN 0-8245-1778-4 (pbk.)
    1. God – Fatherhood. 2. Catholic Church – Doctrines.
I. Theological-Historical Commission for the Grand Jubilee of the
Year 2000.   II. Title.
BT153.F3D5613   1998
231'.1 – dc21   98-39717

1   2   3   4   5   6   7   8   9   10   02   01   00   99   98

Contents

Abbreviations

DM   *Dives in Misericordia,* Rich in Mercy, encyclical letter of John Paul II on divine mercy

DS   *Enchiridion Symbolorum, Definitionum et Declarationum de Rebus Fidei et Morum,* ed. H. Denzinger and A. Schönmetzer (1965)

RM   *Redemptoris Mater,* Mother of the Redeemer, encyclical letter of John Paul II on the Blessed Virgin Mary

TMA   *Tertio Millennio Adveniente,* With the Coming of the Third Millennium, apostolic letter of John Paul II on the Great Jubilee of the Year 2000

TPM II   *Testi del Primo Millennio* (Texts of the First Millennium), vol. 2 (Rome: Città Nova, 1989)

TPM III   *Testi del Primo Millennio* (Texts of the First Millennium), vol. 3 (Rome: Città Nova, 1989)

WA   Martin Luthers Werke. Kritische Gesamtausgabe (Weimar, 1883ff.)

Foreword

To the Father

In the Trinitarian life of God, as in the Christian life of human beings, all things begin with the Father and all things return there. Here is the great cycle revealed and traversed by Jesus Christ, "true God and true human being."

This book ushers us into the third and last year of preparation for the Jubilee of the year 2000. It plunges us into the refreshing waters of the mystery of a God who exists only by and for love. God is Father in the absolute sense of the word. To believe is to recognize God as Father, as our Father. The year 1999 ought to be an immense act of faith in this divine fatherhood, an act of faith that will send us leaping for joy toward the Great Jubilee.

How God loves us! He is the Father who tirelessly covers his prodigal child with his hands, as Rembrandt's portrait shows him. After the first human being's sin, the love of God donned the vesture of mercy. God can no longer love but in forgiving. Indeed, I daresay, God's greatest joy is in forgiving, since the only way in which God can love us is by being merciful, God's only manner of being faithful to his love of the first moment. The human being can cease to be a child of God, but God cannot cease to be our Father. God is infinitely Father, indefinitely Father.

The royal door by which the love of God gushes forth upon us is that of the heart of his Son, pierced on the cross. Here is the holy door, the door of jubilation.

Happy those who, having discovered this wellspring of love, can no longer detach themselves from it!

Happy those who, drinking at this spring of love, see their thirst increase at the very moment of its slaking!

Happy are those who cannot contain their joy, and like wan-

9

dering fools, like pilgrims, race from hill to hill crying out the love of the Father!

Yes, may this book move us to undergo a "joy treatment" — the gladness of a jubilee, as we dare to believe in the love of the Father.

"Lord, show us the Father, and we will be satisfied" (John 14:8).

ROGER CARDINAL ETCHEGARAY
July 22, 1998

Chapter 1

The Names of God

Who is the human being? It is a vexing question for the modern world. Countless responses have been proposed. The human being is the thinker, the artisan, the creator, but also the victim of economic, social, and psychological conditioning. Some regard human beings as constantly called upon to transcend themselves: they recall the myriad wonders of history and culture, as they dream of vanquishing the stars with the help of technology and project a universe of peace and prosperity. Others observe the horrors committed by human beings in their long history, the wages of weakness, war, murder, and slavery. Technological progress has aggravated human beings' cruelty in their relationship with their neighbors, and the sullying of the environment steadily increases. The "realists" emphasize our incredible incapacity to explain ourselves and what we are seeking. So many scholars have devoted so much time and energy to the quest for the truth about the human being, and fail to reach agreement! One has the impression, in the modern world, that philosophers have given up the quest for truth and regard every theory as a smokescreen masking the human being's lowest, most irrational instincts. We can reach the stars, but we cannot live in peace in our own families. All persons desire happiness, but they fail to agree on what it is and, above all, seem incapable of attaining it. Let us see how human beings present themselves in their glory and their misery. Hamlet acknowledged the contradiction that human beings are in themselves:

> What a piece of work is a man! how noble in reason! how infinite in faculty! in form and moving how express and admirable! in action how like an angel! in apprehen-

sion how like a god! the beauty of the world! the paragon
of animals! And yet, to me, what is this quintessence of
dust? (*Hamlet,* act 2, scene 2)

Human beings are a composite of glory and misery, life and
death. Is their glory but arrogance, or their misery but a stim-
ulus to growth? Pascal gave utterance to the dilemma that
human beings are for themselves:

> What a chimera, then, is the human being! What novelty,
> what a monster, what chaos, what a subject of contradic-
> tions, what a prodigy! Judge of all things, and miserable
> worm of earth; depository of truth, and sewer of incerti-
> tude and error! Glory and rejection of the universe! Who
> will ever manage to disentangle this skein? (*Pensées* 164,
> "Contrariétés")

Human beings have need of some response to their questions about the meaning of existence. Without this response,
there is no hope of acting in concord in view of a common
goal, and the basis of societal and civil cooperation is destroyed. If ideological pluralism is invincible, either there will
be endless conflict, or one ideological group will impose its
view on the others. Without the light of reason, human beings
will lose their path in an ever murkier forest. Human beings
are still a mystery to themselves. If they are to rely solely upon
themselves in order to understand themselves, they are doomed
to frustration. Their mystery can be grasped only in the light of
a greater mystery. Thus, human beings have always looked to
God to answer their questions about themselves.

Ancient civilizations were well aware of human beings' limi-
tations, and their helplessness to solve their own problems and
realize their own hopes. They observed that even the best laid
plans frequently went uncrowned with success — that great
empires crumbled, and that next month the harvest could lie
waste. In the vastness of the universe, the human being was

awash in meaninglessness. Greek poet Homer lamented, with profound insight:

> Very like leaves
> upon this earth are the generations of men —
> old leaves, cast on the ground by wind, young leaves
> the greening forest bears when spring comes in.
> So mortals pass; one generation flowers
> even as another dies away.
>
> (*The Iliad,* book 6, ll. 146–49)

The simile truly shows the insignificance and tragedy of human life. After the wind has swept the leaves away, spring creates them anew; but the human being is born and dies. If, then, human reality falls like leaves swept by the wind, without the new youth of spring, there is no hope of finding a definitive response to the questions that disturb humankind. Thus, instead of observing impermanent, precarious human reality, the ancients regarded the divine. "Who is God?" was their central question when it came to the meaning of existence. Nearly all of them were in agreement that, just the contrary of human mutability and mortality, the divine was deathless and abiding.

After this initial agreement, humanity's various conceptions of the divine were frequently in mutual conflict. What is the divine? Many regarded the universe itself as divine. True, it had existed, with its unhurried cycles, before human beings, and it gave every impression that it would continue to exist after the current generation had returned to dust. But in what form would the divine be manifested? Some looked to nature, with its rhythmic recurrence of the seasons. Nature offered a fundamental stability to the orderly flow of human life. Others looked to the stars, and found there, in their recurrent cycles, the guide for human action. But what is the human relationship with the divine? Is the divine personal? Does the divinity exercise care of human beings? Since human beings have only visible creation to guide their mind and their imagination, and visible creation is so ambiguous, a variety of opinions arose.

There were divine forces governing the world, and the human being must take these into account. Human beings sought to control them or propitiate them, in such a way that these forces would support their undertakings and guarantee their success.

Since human endeavors so frequently ended in failure, mortals understood that it was not easy to control the divinity. The universe seemed a battlefield, on which numerous hostile forces were to be met, and human beings found themselves torn in their very being by conflictive desires. Now they were driven by a tender piety, now by rage, and then suddenly by passion followed by remorse. Gold attracted some, power others, knowledge still others. Human beings did not always know what they wanted, as the imperious forces of the universe continued their struggle within them. Not surprisingly, in order to explain this tumultuous mixture of desires and forces, a multitude of divinities were imagined. These aroused their desires, just as they struggled to control the external course of events in the universe. Since there were so many gods to be propitiated, the human being lived in fear of inadvertently neglecting one or the other. The great epic poets Homer and Virgil sang of the fate of Troy and its consequences, in which so many persons were destroyed because they were caught up in the rivalry of the gods. The great Greek tragedian Aeschylus portrayed the tragic lot of the family of Agamemnon, constrained to pay the price of a vindictive justice based on the principle of tit for tat where various gods and goddesses were concerned, at the close of the Trojan War. Euripides recounts the wretched end of Hippolytus. In his desire to serve the chaste goddess Artemis, he came into conflict with the goddess of sex, Aphrodite, who unleashed her own vendetta upon him and the house of his father. Again, the pagans were very concerned with prayer in the sense of addressing the divinity with all of its various titles, lest a single one be omitted, which would entail the risk of not being heard, or, worse, of arousing the divine anger. Jesus was referring to the sorrowful lot of pagan humanity when he said to his disciples: "When you are praying, do not heap up empty phrases as the Gentiles do" (Matt. 6:7). Instead, he taught his disciples to pray, in all simplicity, the Our Father (Matt. 6:9–13). For Christians, God is revealed as their merciful Father.

What Is in a Name?

Jesus could instruct his disciples in this fashion because, as Jews, they were the depositories of a long tradition of faith in one God and Lord. When God called Abram from Mesopotamia, from Ur of the Chaldeans and Haran, Abram left his country, his kinsfolk, and even his father's house, to serve God alone. Thereby opened a new era in the history of humanity. Abram was destined to be a blessing for all of the families of the earth. From his loins would issue a new people, entirely consecrated to the Lord (Gen. 11:31–12:5). In exchange for Abram's fidelity, God struck a covenant with him, promising him a great destiny. This new relationship was so decisive that God changed Abram's name: "As for me, this is my covenant with you: You shall be the ancestor of a multitude of nations. No longer shall your name be Abram, but your name shall be Abraham; for I have made you the ancestor of a multitude of nations" (Gen. 17:4–5). While Abram (Abraham) is actually only a dialectical variant of Abram, which means "the [divine] father is exalted," its similarity in Hebrew with "father of a multitude" indicates the importance of the covenant. At first, however, God's design was concentrated on the immediate descendants of Abraham. The Old Testament tells the story of God's interventions, in the divine confrontations with the chosen people, in preparing that people for the final revelation of God in the divine Son: "Long ago God spoke to our ancestors in many and various ways by the prophets, but in these last days he has spoken to us by a Son, whom he appointed heir of all things, through whom he also created the worlds" (Heb. 1:1–2). The divine revelation occurred gradually in time.

Only through time can persons learn who God is and who they themselves are called to be.

For the ancient human being, names were of crucial importance. Names gave each person an identity among the others and before God. A person's name usually took account of the father who had generated the child. Not only was the baby known as "son of" or "daughter of" the father, but the latter also transmitted his own name to the offspring. In the ancient Middle East, a victorious king frequently imposed by treaty a new name on a defeated king, to show that the latter belonged to him as a vassal. Thus, when God changed Abram's name to Abraham, Sarai's to Sara, and Jacob's to Israel, this act indicated that God was granting them a blessing, or establishing a special relationship with them. God was taking them under the divine protection, and the persons in question were to honor God as their own Lord (Gen. 27:5, 15; 32:28). In similar fashion, the Suffering Servant proclaimed that God had called him by name from his mother's womb, thereby declaring that God had chosen him to belong to God in a special way: God had assigned him a task, and he was under the divine protection (Isa. 49:12–6). Similarly, Jeremiah and Saint Paul retraced their divine call to the maternal womb (Jer. 1:5–10; Gal. 1:15–16). Again, Jesus changed Simon's name to Peter to indicate the function that he would discharge in the Church (Matt. 16:17–19). In analogous fashion, in the Church infants receive their name when they are baptized in Christ, God become a human being to save them and to show them what it truly means that the human being is the image of God. They become children of God in the Son.

The Names of God

As with the names of human beings, great importance attaches to God's name, as well. God's personal identity is expressed in the divine name. In antiquity, it was thought that knowledge of a person's name imparted a certain power over the person. For this reason, after the struggle between God and Jacob, which led to the change in the name Jacob to Israel, God refused to reveal the divine name (Gen. 32:29–30; cf. Judg. 13:17–19). Times were not yet ripe; Jacob was not yet ready. It is not that God was without a name. The Old Testament attributed them to him in abundance. Their very multiplicity revealed something of the divine mystery. Indeed, one name did not enable a person to identify God fully. On the other hand, each name revealed something of the manner in which God was gradually making a self-revelation to human beings. Frequently God is called *'El.* In the language of the Semites, *'El* meant simply "God." It could be applied to any one of the multitude of gods and failed to distinguish one from another. Customarily, a further distinction was applied in order to specify what God was being referred to. The goddess or god could be individuated through the indication of the place where this divinity appeared, or where a place of worship had been built in his or her honor (e.g., Bethel, Gen. 35:7). Or a divinity could be identified through an indication of his or her devotees. God was known as the god of Abraham, Isaac, and Jacob, because he had appeared to them and they had worshiped him. God was known, then, through the divine apparitions of history and through the divinely chosen people.

Probably owing to the indeterminacy of the expression *'El,* the ancient Israelites, who knew the supremacy of their God over all others, sought to express this preeminence with the term *'Elohim.* This title introduced an exceptional grammatical usage. Although *'Elohim* is plural in form, it is followed by a verb in the singular when it denotes the God of Israel. Thus, the plural form of the substantive suggests an intensification, or even an absolutization, of the divinity — somewhat like "God of gods," or "supreme God." The God of Israel brooks no strange gods before his face (Exod. 20:2–3).

In the fundamental covenant with Abraham, God made a self-proclamation as *'El-Shaddai,* the "almighty God." Although this name separated this God from all others, who are less mighty, God later told Moses that he had appeared to the patriarchs only as *'El-Shaddai,* and "by my name 'the Lord' [YHWH] I did not make myself known to them" (Exod. 6:3). God's interior reality, then, involves a deeper mystery. This is how God emphasized the meaning and novelty of this self-revelation to Moses in the burning bush. Here for the first time, the God of the ancestors, of Abraham, Isaac, and Jacob, was identified with a name that was a derivative neither of a generic Semitic designation of the divinity, nor one of a divine characteristic replacing a name. When Moses asked God the name of the God of the Fathers of Israel, he received this reply. "I AM WHO I AM. . . . Thus you shall say to the Israelites, 'I AM has sent me to you. . . . The Lord, the God of your ancestors, the God of Abraham, the God of Isaac, and the God of Jacob, has sent me to you.' This is my name forever, and this my title for all generations" (Exod 3:14–15).

God's name in Hebrew is YHWH. It expresses God's great sanctity, but it does not indicate an altogether transcendent God. Even the self-revelation to Moses was clearly linked not only to him, as God's greatest prophet, but also to the great historical actions with which Israel had been delivered from the slavery of Egypt and constituted a special people among all of the peoples of the earth. Through Moses, God speaks to Israel thus:

> I am the Lord [YHWH], and I will free you from the burdens of the Egyptians and deliver you from slavery to them. I will redeem you with an outstretched arm and with mighty acts of judgment. I will take you as my people, and I will be your God. You shall know that I am the Lord your God, who has freed you from the burdens of the Egyptians. I will bring you into the land that I swore to give to Abraham, Isaac, and Jacob; I will give it to you for a possession. I am the Lord. (Exod. 6:6–8)

Ineluctably, the revelation of the name of God was more than just one more piece of information among so many others. In this self-revelation, God adopted a people, a people called to worship God and to be delivered. God tolerated no neutrality. The divine choice was at the origin of the human being's response. Just as the Mosaic covenant represented a fuller realization of the covenant struck with Abraham, so also the New Covenant, in the blood of Our Lord Jesus Christ, has sealed the realization and the transcendence of the Old with God's final revelation, the constitution of a new people and its deliverance from sin. Writing at the conclusion of the New Testament, Saint John proclaims, with the greatest imaginable clarity, the mysterious reality of God: "God is love" (1 John 4:8, 16). This new designation is not an abstraction a philosopher might predicate of the divine essence, in the sense that God is love of self as the supreme Good. Instead, for Saint John God is the Father who exists in eternal relationship with the Son and the Holy Spirit. Indeed, God the Father can be love only because God is Father, Son, and Holy Spirit. As tripersonal, God gives a new meaning, the divine meaning, to love, and shows human beings the image in which they have been created.

In Jesus, God has been revealed as a Father who loves, and who desires to reconcile all human beings to the divine self. "Father" is not a name invented by human beings to designate somehow, by way of an analogy with human begetting, the ineffable, creative mystery in the background of the universe. Rather, "Father" is God's self-revelation, in view of which the universe has been created. As Saint Paul wrote: "I bow my knees before the Father, from whom every family in heaven and on earth takes its name" (Eph. 3:14–15). Human beings have become children of God only because God is the original Parent, and any parenthood has meaning only to the extent that it reflects the loving mystery of the Origin of all things in heaven and on earth. "Father," then, reveals, altogether profoundly, who God is, and reveals to human beings their calling.

Chapter 2

God the Father

God is a mystery of love, Trinitarian love. The Father loves the Son in the bond of the Holy Spirit, who is their reciprocal love. This central mystery of Christianity is the source and the end of all of the other mysteries, and of all that has life in the Church. Accordingly, the only way in which we know the eternal mystery of the Trinity is through the deed of our salvation accomplished in Jesus Christ, God's only Son. After all, our salvation consists in sharing the very life of the Trinity. What has been revealed in the sacred Scriptures is not for the satisfaction of our intellectual curiosity. It has been revealed for our salvation (2 Tim. 3:15–16).

The mystery of the Incarnation involved the entire Trinity. The Father sent the angel Gabriel to announce to Mary the birth of an infant. He would be called the "Son of the Most High" (Luke 1:32). The human generation or begetting of the "Son of God" will then occur by the work of the Holy Spirit (Luke 26:31–32, 35; Matt. 1:18, 20; Gal. 4:4–6). At the inception of Jesus' public life the mystery of the Trinity is revealed again, this time openly, to all. After Jesus had been baptized by John, the Holy Spirit descended on him in the form of a dove, and the voice of the Father proclaimed: "This is my Son, the Beloved, with whom I am well pleased" (Matt. 3:17). John the Baptizer was full of the Holy Spirit from his mother's womb (Luke 1:15) and proclaimed the coming of one who would be baptized in the Holy Spirit (Luke 3:16; Mark 1:8–11). Thus, he was fully capable of recognizing the Holy Spirit, who was descending and resting upon Jesus, and therefore could testify that Jesus was the "Son of God" (John 1:32–34).

The conclusion of Jesus' earthly ministry corresponds to its beginning. The Gospel according to Matthew ends with the account of the ongoing mission entrusted by Jesus to his disciples:

All authority in heaven and on earth has been given to me. Go therefore and make disciples of all nations, baptizing them in the name of the Father and of the Son and of the Holy Spirit, and teaching them to obey everything that I have commanded you. And remember, I am with you always, to the end of the age. (Matt. 28:18–20)

Jesus had received his authority from the Father. His object was to reveal the mystery of God. This is what he asserted with the words: "All things have been handed over to me by my Father; and no one knows the Son except the Father, and no one knows the Father except the Son and anyone to whom the Son chooses to reveal him" (Matt. 11:27). Reporting this same statement by the Lord, Luke couches it in the following context: "At that same hour Jesus rejoiced in the Holy Spirit and said:..." (Luke 10:21). In this fashion, Luke was declaring that the public profession of the Father on Jesus' part had been professed in the Holy Spirit. Father, Son, and Holy Spirit are united in the work of revelation and redemption. Only under the action of the Spirit can believers confess Jesus as Lord and recognize in the Son the face of their merciful Father (1 Cor. 12:3; John 14:9). As Jesus' public life commenced at his baptism by John with a manifestation of the mystery of the Trinity, so also the deed of salvation after his resurrection continues in the power of God one and three. Jesus' work, which consists in proclaiming the love of the Father in the power of the Holy Spirit, continues in his Church. Here, through baptism, his disciples communicate the Trinitarian life to all believers.

The first Christian communities were charged with the Trinitarian life. At the end of his Second Letter to the Corinthians, Saint Paul writes: "The grace of the Lord Jesus Christ, the love of God, and the communion of the Holy Spirit be with all of

you" (2 Cor. 13:13). With this concluding phrase, he recapit-
ulates the recurring themes of his letters: Christians are led to
share the life of God the Father through his Son, Jesus Christ,
in the Holy Spirit.

God the Father in Creation

> Blessed be the God and Father of our Lord Jesus Christ,
> who has blessed us in Christ with every spiritual bless-
> ing in the heavenly places, just as he chose us in Christ
> before the foundation of the world to be holy and blame-
> less before him in love. He destined us for adoption as
> his children through Jesus Christ, according to the good
> pleasure of his will, to the praise of his glorious grace
> that he freely bestowed on us in the Beloved. In him we
> have redemption through his blood, the forgiveness of
> our trespasses, according to the riches of his grace that he
> lavished on us. With all wisdom and insight he has made
> known to us the mystery of his will, according to his good
> pleasure that he set forth in Christ, as a plan for the full-
> ness of time, to gather up all things in him, in heaven and
> things on earth. (Eph. 1:3–10; cf. Col. 1:11–20)

This text permits us to assert, first of all, that, in formulating
the divine plan of salvation, God the Father was never alone.
The Son was always with him. Before his death, Jesus prayed:
"So now, Father, glorify me in your own presence with the
glory that I had in your presence before the world existed"
(John 17:5). In the exordium of his Gospel, too, John asserted:
"In the beginning was the Word, and the Word was with God,
and the Word was God. All things came into being with him,
and without him not one thing came into being" (John 1:1–3).
In the same fashion, Paul has described Christ as mediator of
creation: "For us there is one God, the Father, from whom are
all things and for whom we exist, and one Lord, Jesus Christ,

through whom are all things and through whom we exist"
(1 Cor. 8:6).

In God's plan, all things come from the Father through the
Son, and are to return to the Father through the Son. Speaking
of the final resurrection, when all human beings will rise again
in Christ, Saint Paul writes:

> For as all die in Adam, so all will be made alive in Christ.
> But each in his own order: Christ the first fruits, then at
> his coming those who belong to Christ. Then comes the
> end, when he hands over the kingdom to God the Father,
> after he has destroyed every ruler and every authority and
> power. For he must reign until he has put all his enemies
> under his feet. The last enemy to be destroyed is death.
> For "God has put all things in subjection under his feet."
> But when it says, "All things are put in subjection," it is
> plain that this does not include the one who put all things
> in subjection under him. When all things are subjected to
> him, then the Son himself will also be subjected to the one
> who put all things in subjection under him, so that God
> may be all in all. (1 Cor. 15:22–28)

The same mediation of Christ is taken up once more in the Letter to the Colossians, with its description of the role of Christ
in the deed of salvation:

> He is the image of the invisible God, the firstborn of all
> creation; for in him all things in heaven and on earth
> were created, things visible and invisible, whether thrones
> or dominions or rulers or powers — all things have been
> created through him and for him. He himself is before
> all things, and in him all things hold together. He is the
> head of the body, the church; he is the beginning, the first-
> born from the dead, so that he might come to have first
> place in everything. For in him all the fullness of God
> was pleased to dwell, and through him God was pleased
> to reconcile to himself all things, whether on earth or in

heaven, by making peace through the blood of his cross.
(Col. 1:15–20)

Authority of the Father

What is the relationship between the Father and the Son? Obviously neither is more or less divine than the other: both are fully and authentically divine. Still, the Father and the Son must not be imagined as simply identical persons. There is true diversity within the divinity. While some medieval artistic representations pictured the three persons of the Trinity as identical figures, this attempt to emphasize the equality of their divinity failed to do complete justice to the personal diversity within the infinite mystery of the Trinitarian love.

A great help for our reflection is offered by Saint Hilary in his discussion of the text that was so familiar by reason of its use by the Arians: "The Father is greater than I" (John 14:28). The bishop of Poitiers sees, in this expression, a very profound meaning. Granted, he maintains, in the economy of salvation the Son has become less than the Father, seeing that his divine nature was emptied of its "form" as it took the form of a slave, becoming obedient to the very death. In return for this obedience, the Father reestablished the Son in equality of form, and gave him a name above every other name, restoring him as Son, one with himself in his glory (Phil. 2:6–11). The Father is greater, Hilary continues, by his "authority," in bestowing the divine name on the Son and in glorifying him. Thus Jesus' words, "The Father and I are one [thing]," remain true, since Jesus is in the glory of the Father. "The bestower is greater, but the one to whom it is granted to be one thing with him is not lesser." Indeed, Hilary realized that what had been accomplished and revealed in the economy of salvation, in the incarnation, death, resurrection, and ascension of the Son, applied also to the eternal relation of the Father and the Son. As Father, God has a greater authority; but this does not make the Son less. "The Father is greater than the Son, and surely greater, since He allows Himself to be as great as He Himself is" and gives all that he himself is. But, once more, the Son, who possesses the nature of the Father, and the Father's being, in the eternal generation and begetting, is not the less for all that. "From the fact that the Father is greater, understand the acknowledgment of the Father's authority!"[1]

Hilary derives his argumentation from the word *auctoritas*. This Latin term is translated, literally, "authority." In many persons, today, the word arouses resistance on account of its use in recent history. The European Enlightenment, for example, claimed to deliver human beings from all tutelage and imposition, in such a way that they might be able autonomously to see and decide what was true and right. Thus, it rejected all sources of authority outside of one's own "I." This orientation favored the abandonment of all traditions and the isolation of the individual from society. The individual was called to follow his or her own path in the world, and to dominate that world. But, with time, extreme individualism gave rise to alienation and simultaneously provoked the opposite extreme: a totalitarian collectivism in which individuals found their own meaning only in the group, whose unity was maintained by the "authority" of an ideology or a charismatic leader. Naturally, the excesses and bankruptcies of these authoritarian regimes, whether fascist, socialist, or communist, have confirmed the peremptory rejection of "authoritarianism" in any and every form; just so, today, certain feminist ideologies reject all paternal authority or role, defining it as paternalistic and authoritarian.

We live in an age that has attacked the very notion of fatherhood and that vaunts its own rebellion against authority. By "authority," Hilary did not mean primarily an imposition from without. *Auctoritas,* in the Latin of his time, could surely

---

1. Hilary of Poitiers, *De Trinitate,* book 9, nos. 52–56; book 11, no. 12; *PL* 10:325A–327B, 407C; Eng. trans.: *The Trinity,* trans. Stephen McKenna, C.SS.R., The Fathers of the Church: A New Translation 25 (Washington, D.C.: Catholic University of America Press, 1954), 377, 469.

denote power, or even a juridical decree; but it also had a much broader denotation. Basically, it manifested the quality of being an *auctor*. This Latin word denotes a "progenitor," a "parent," or a "forebear" in the proper sense of the one who gives existence to another, enhancing that other's well-being and prosperity. It designated, then, something very positive. As good parents not only give their offspring life, but sustain them in growth with a personal love as well, so, for Hilary, the authority of God the Father over the Son was not an imposed, extraneous condition, but the authority of love. It derived from the very communication of the nature and being of the Father to the Son. After all, the actual nature of God is love.

Saint Hilary's conception can help us better understand the central mystery of Christian love. There can be no question of the interior life of God abiding as a mere static identity in which the divine persons are frozen in a state of immobility. God's life is abundant, infinite, overflowing. If the Christian measure is "good, ... pressed down, shaken together, running over" (Luke 6:38), does not this measure find its model and norm in God, who is the All-Merciful? The interior of God is an infinite interchange within, an ongoing self-bestowal between Father and Son in the Holy Spirit. The Father gives all of the divinity to the Son, and the latter restores the same to the Father. There is no danger, in this reciprocal exchange, of a loss of the divine self on either side, nor any need to have recourse to violence in order to overcome evil: the gift can be and is without reserve, as reciprocation.

In God's free infinitude, there is no limit in the act of giving. Our language risks becoming a stammer when we seek to describe the reality of God. In God there is no real distinction between "being" and "having." The Father does not simply *have* divinity; the Father *is* divinity, which is shared with the Son utterly. As Hilary noted, the Father "gives all that is himself." The Council of Florence would define the community of life between Father, Son, and Holy Spirit in the following way: "These three persons are one God, not three gods, because of the three the substance is one, one the essence, one the nature, one the divinity, one the immensity, one the eternity, and all things are one thing, where there is no opposition of relation" (DS 1330). The Father makes such a whole gift of self that only the to-be-Father is not given — since if it were possible for the Father to abandon fatherhood itself, there would be no Son to receive the eternal gift of divinity. We can see this mystery reflected in the gift of parents to their children. We say that parents give everything they have to their children: their time, their energy, their goods, their attention, their care. Actually, they are giving themselves, to the limit of their capacity to do so. This is particularly evident in the case of the mother, who gives a child life and body — and even, at times, in imitation of the Trinitarian love, sacrifices her very life in order that her child may come into the world. Indeed, recently the Church has acknowledged the validity of this form of love by beatifying Gianna Beretta Molla, who, suffering from a tumor of the uterus, freely chose to die so that her daughter might be born.

God's Self-Emptying

This reciprocal exchange of life, love, and being among the persons of the Most Holy Trinity explains certain difficult texts of the New Testament. Having described how the Good Shepherd gives his own life for the sheep, Jesus goes on: "For this reason the Father loves me, because I lay down my life to take it up again. No one takes it from me, but I lay it down of my own accord. I have power to lay it down, and I have power to take it up again. I have received this command from my Father" (John 10:17–18).

It is erroneous to interpret this passage as if the Father loved Jesus only because Jesus offers his life on the cross — as if he must somehow win the Father's love. On the contrary, the revelation of Jesus in this world reflects who Jesus is eternally. In the eternal Trinity itself, he gives his own life entirely and freely to the Father, and — such is the mystery of love — in giv-

ing himself he takes up his own life anew. Precisely in virtue of
this experience of his, Jesus could tell his disciples: "Those who
want to save their life will lose it, and those who lose their life
for my sake, and for the sake of the gospel, will save it" (Mark
8:35; cf. John 12:24–26).

The mystery of the Trinity also explains the mystery of
Jesus' death on the cross. In the famous hymn of the Letter
to the Philippians, Saint Paul proclaims:

> Let the same mind be in you that was in Christ Jesus,
> who, though he was in the form of God,
> did not regard equality with God
> as something to be exploited,
> but emptied himself,
> taking the form of a slave,
> being born in human likeness.
> And being found in human form,
> he humbled himself
> and became obedient to the point of death —
> even death on a cross.
> Therefore God also highly exalted him
> and gave him the name
> that is above every name,
> so that at the name of Jesus
> every knee should bend,
> in heaven and on earth and under the earth,
> and every tongue should confess
> that Jesus Christ is Lord,
> to the glory of God the Father. (Phil. 2:5–11)

Jesus' self-emptying on the cross is not anything contrary
or contradictory to his divinity. Rather, it reveals his divinity,
which consists in the love that gives itself fully. In the eternal
Trinity itself, Jesus had already emptied himself: he had lost
himself in the Father, to be able to find himself once more
and be fully himself. His self-emptying on the cross, then,

is nothing but the revelation in our history of who God is: self-giving Love.

This understanding of Trinitarian Love, in which the Son returns his own being and his own nature to the Father as his origin, also explains why Jesus could say: "Come to me, all you that are weary and are carrying heavy burdens, and I will give you rest. Take my yoke upon you, and learn from me; for I am gentle and humble in heart, and you will find rest for your souls. For my yoke is easy, and my burden is light" (Matt. 11:28–30).

Declarations of this sort were scandalous to the ancient world. Never before had humility been considered a virtue. Aristotle, the great Athenian philosopher, regarded it out and out as a vice: a humble person had no sense of self-worth (*Nicomachean Ethics* 4, 3, 1125A 19–28). And yet because God is humble, Saint Paul enjoins Christians to be humble. Obviously this divine humility must not be restricted to Jesus' earthly life: inasmuch as Jesus receives all from the Father, he knows that he has nothing of his own. As Saint Hilary put it: "The Son is not the author of his own being, nor, not existing, did he go in quest of his own birth from nothing" (*De Trinitate,* 9, 53, *PL* 10:324A). All is given to him as gift. He has no need of claiming it as his own; he need only accept all from the Father, with gratitude. This humility is the very reason for his exaltation.

In her own turn, the Virgin Mary was able to demonstrate the truth underlying Christian humility. Because God has "looked with favor on the lowliness of his servant," Mary's spirit "rejoices in God," her Savior. The almighty God who "has scattered the proud in the thoughts of their hearts ... and lifted up the lowly," has done "great things" in his mercy. And so "from now on all generations will call *me* blessed" (Luke 1:47–52). Precisely because she knew she had not actually deserved God's favor, and did not have the right to God's mercy, Mary must rejoice in her exaltation. Love must always be a free gift.

If the Trinity can be understood as a mystery of self-emptying love, perhaps the reason for the Holy Spirit's "facelessness" becomes clear. The Spirit exists as common Spirit of the Father and the Son, the Spirit of Love. The Spirit desires anonymity, because its only care is for the unification of the Father and the Son, not for itself. In some sense, in the Holy Spirit the divinity shows its most radiant perfection: here it is pure self-emptying, in anonymity. And yet it is the Spirit of Love which best characterizes the entire Trinity as Love. Losing itself in the Father and in the Son, the Spirit finds itself in the Father and in the Son: not by insisting on its own rights to adoration and praise, nor even on its relevance in history, but as altogether glad to be where it is — infinitely lost in the Father and the Son, and more itself, more gladsome, when the Father and the Son glorify one another in it.

Chapter 3

Jesus Reveals the Father

The Human Being Created in the Image of God

The object of creation, as declared in the Letter to the Ephesians (1:4–5), evinces our summons to be children of God. Let us recall the account from the Book of Genesis.

Then God said, "Let us make humankind in our image, according to our likeness; and let them have dominion over the fish of the sea, and over the birds of the air, and over the cattle, and over all of the wild animals of the earth, and over every creeping thing that creeps upon the earth."

So God created humankind in his image,
in the image of God he created them;
male and female he created them.

God blessed them, and God said to them, "Be fruitful and multiply, and fill the earth and subdue it; and have dominion over the fish of the sea and over the birds of the air and over every living thing that moves upon the earth." God said, "See, I have given you every plant yielding seed that is upon the face of all the earth, and every tree with seed in its fruit; you shall have them for food. And to every beast of the earth, and to every bird of the air, and to everything that creeps on the earth, everything that has the breath of life, I have given every green plant for food." And it was so. God saw everything that he had made, and indeed, it was very good. And there was evening and there was morning, the sixth day.

Thus the heavens and the earth were finished, and all their multitude. And on the seventh day God finished the

work that he had done, and he rested on the seventh day
from all the work that he had done. So God blessed the
seventh day and hallowed it, because on it God rested
from all the work that he had done in creation.

(Gen. 1:26–2:3)

The sixth day represented the pinnacle of God's creative
deed, before he began, on the seventh day, his rest from his
work. The sacred writer desired to emphasize, by citing this
repose, this *Sabbath,* that God is Lord of the divine creation.
Creation does not consist in some kind of perpetual motion
machine, and is not finished once for all, as if God withdrew
from the world and let it follow its own course. The world
remains completely and continuously dependent on the divine
power. All is maintained and accomplished in God's "rest"
even after the initial summons from nothingness: indeed, the
eternal Son is the one who "sustains all things by his powerful word" (Heb. 1:3; cf. Wisd. 11:25). As Jesus has said: "My
Father is still working, and I also am working" (John 5:17).
Commenting on these words of Our Lord, Saint Augustine observed that creatures would cease to exist "if He who made
creatures ceased to exercise His provident rule over them."[2]

The sacred writer did not primarily wish to stress the contin-
gency of creation. Rather he was considering the miracle of the
origin of human beings, and marveling at their destiny. During
the week, human beings would have charge of creation, but
on the seventh day they were invited to anticipate God's full
lordship, symbolized by the divine "rest."

The human being, then, was created "in the divine image
and likeness." This is said of no other creature. Indeed, while
it is true that all of the other works of creation are judged
"good" by God at the end of each day, only after the creation of the human being did God pronounce the superlative,

---

2. *De Genesi ad Litteram,* book 5, chap. 20; *PL* 34:335. Eng. trans.: Johannes
Quasten, et al., eds., *St. Augustine: The Literal Meaning of Genesis,* vol. 1, books
1–6, trans. John Hammond Taylor, S.J., Ancient Christian Writers: The Works of
the Fathers in Translation, 1:172.

"very good." With the human being, creation had reached its completion, and thereafter God could "rest." After all, God had made a creature in the divine image, a creature that reflected its creator. In what does this reflection or image consist? It is interesting to observe that, in describing the object of God's creative concern, the sacred writer has passed from the singular, "humankind," literally, "human being," to the plural: "male and female." The double expression connotes, in God's presence, the completeness and fullness of the human race. No human being *exists* in isolation. Unless we had had parents, we should not exist. Had we not been loved, nourished, and taught to speak, we should be incapable of speaking and communicating reciprocally. Thus, from the human being's inception, as female and male, she and he exist in fertile communion, and for a later communication within the mystery of God's creative love.

The notion of "image of God" has been subjected to various interpretations in the history of the Church. From the very beginning, a Christological exegesis of the expression was proposed. Saint Paul defined Christ as the "image of God" (2 Cor. 4:4) and at once connected this image with the new creation: "For we do not proclaim ourselves; we proclaim Jesus Christ as Lord and ourselves as your slaves for Jesus' sake. For it is God who said, 'Let light shine out of darkness,' who has shone in our hearts to give the light of the knowledge of the glory of God in the face of Jesus Christ" (2 Cor. 4:5–6).

Likewise in the Letter to the Colossians Paul acknowledges Christ as the "image of the invisible God, the firstborn of all creation" and recalls to Christians that they have put on the "new self, which is being renewed in knowledge according to the image of its creator" (Col. 1:15; 3:10).

The Gospel of Saint John, as well, in slightly different language, develops a like theme when it identifies Jesus with the *Logos* of God, who has always been divine, who is the creator of all things, who has shone like light in the darkness, and who has become incarnate for our salvation (John 1:1–5,

14). As Word and Thought of the Father, Jesus clearly reflects and reveals the Father. In response to Philip's request to show him the Father, Jesus says: "Have I been with you all this time, Philip, and you still do not know me? Whoever has seen me has seen the Father. How can you say, 'Show us the Father'? Do you not believe that I am in the Father and the Father is in me?" (John 14:9–10).

In the same fashion as Saint Paul stresses that Christ reveals the invisible God, Saint John evidences the identical mystery: "No one has ever seen God. It is God the only Son, who is close to the Father's heart, who has made him known" (John 1:18).

The Christological interpretation was current among the Fathers. Against the Gnostic heresy, which excessively spiritualized the human being and disdained the human body, Saint Irenaeus and his successors insisted that the entire human being, body and soul, is made in the image of God and through Christ is destined for the resurrection of the body for eternal life with God. The human being is called to grow from the image of God to the likeness to God, that is, to the full stature of Christ, who leads human beings to the Father through the mystery of his glorified flesh.

Various passages from the Fathers are a help to us in assimilating this viewpoint. "Actually, the human being is a mixture of soul and flesh modeled on the image of God, and fashioned by the Hands of God, that is, by the Son and the Spirit, to whom he said, 'Let us make the human being,'" wrote Saint Irenaeus. Novatian and Tertullian regard the whole Trinity as at work in creation. Similarly, Saint Athanasius and Saint Hilary interpret God's creative design, "Let us make humankind in our image, according to our likeness," as referring to the Trinity.[3]

3. Saint Irenaeus, *Adversus Haereses,* 4, praef., 4; *PG* 7:958B; Novatian, *De Trinitate,* 17, 26; *PL* 3:917C–918A, 936C; Tertullian, *Adversus Praxean,* 12; *PL* 2:167C–168A; Athanasius, *Contra Arianos,* 3, 29; *PG* 26:387A; Saint Hilary, *De Trinitate,* 4, 17–20; *PL* 10:110A–112B.

God, the Father of Israel

The Old Testament acknowledges God as Father, but the parenthood involved was never extended to all of the persons over the face of the earth. That persons would be children of God depends not on their birth, or their nature, but on God's choice. Israel is recognized as God's Son and firstborn, because God has selected that people among all nations as his own property. At the time of the deliverance from slavery in Egypt, God sends Pharaoh a message: "Thus says the Lord: Israel is my firstborn son. I said to you, 'Let my son go that he may worship me'" (Exod. 4:22–23). Moses was to recall to the people, as well, that God had established a special relationship with them: "Is he not your father, who created you, who made you and established you?" (Deut. 32:6).

The same themes were then repeated by the prophets. Hosea reports the oracle of God: "When Israel was a child, I loved him, and out of Egypt I called my son" (Hos. 11:1). Jeremiah presents YHWH as turning to his people and saying, "I have become a father to Israel, and Ephraim is my firstborn" (Jer. 31:9; cf. 3:14, 22; Mal. 1:6). Isaiah reestablishes the connection between election and creative action: "Yet, O Lord, you are our Father; we are the clay, and you are our potter; we are all the work of your hand" (Isa. 64:8; cf. 63:16). At times the people of Israel are treated as a single offspring; at other times, all of the Israelites are regarded as "children of the living God" (Hos. 1:10; cf. Deut. 14:1; Isa. 1:2; 30:1, 9). The oracles that express God's parenthood by election underscore either God's affectionate care for the chosen people, or the responsibility of the people in the divine sight.

Besides the people in its entirety, the king, as well, who represented the people before God, was called the offspring of God. The divine prophecy proclaimed to David by Nathan regarding David's progeny promised:

> The Lord declares to you that the Lord will make you
> a house. When your days are fulfilled and you lie down

with your ancestors, I will raise up your offspring after you, who shall come forth from your body, and I will establish his kingdom. He shall build a house for my name, and I will establish the throne of his kingdom forever. I will be a father to him, and he shall be a son to me. When he commits iniquity, I will punish him with a rod such as mortals use, with blows inflicted by human beings. But I will not take my steadfast love from him, as I took it from Saul, whom I put away from before you. Your house and your kingdom shall be made sure forever before me; your throne shall be established forever. (2 Sam. 7:11–16; cf. 1 Cor. 17:10–14; 22:8–10; 28:6–7)

This concept of the divine filiation is likewise rooted in Psalm 2, which is sung during the rite of the enthronement of a king: "I will tell of the decree of the Lord: He said to me, 'You are my son; today I have begotten you'" (Ps. 2:7). Although the coronation ceremony apparently borrows a great deal from similar Egyptian rites, the king of Israel, unlike the pharaoh, who was regarded as having been physically generated by a god, was chosen by YHWH. On this basis, a loyalty and confidence were established such that the king could turn to YHWH with trust in difficult moments: "He shall cry to me, 'You are my Father, my God, and the Rock of my salvation!' I will make him the firstborn, the highest of the kings of the earth" (Ps. 89:26–27)

Again, various groups or individuals within the complex of the people of Israel could be called children of God. This is what the psalmist calls the just (73:15), and Malachi addresses the priests, designating them as children of God (Mal. 1:6; 2:10). In the Book of Wisdom, the just, who follow the law of God and practice justice, regard God as their very Father and themselves as "children of the Lord" (Wisd. 2:12–18). Nonetheless, the divine filiation does not attach to the human being by nature or right; it depends instead on God's gratuitous choice of a human being who already exists.

Witness of the New Testament

The New Testament confutes in a still more surprising manner the Enlightenment thesis of the universal condition of human beings' divine filiation. Its testimony acknowledges a single child of God by nature: Jesus Christ, our Lord. Saint John testifies to him as *Logos,* God, and as "a father's only son, full of grace and truth" (John 1:14; cf. 1:18). This grace and this truth are reserved to believers, who *become* children of God by joining themselves to Jesus in faith and love. "To all who received him, who believed in his name, he gave power to become children of God, who were born, not of blood or of the will of the flesh or of the will of man, but of God" (1:12–13). This passage clearly anticipates the "rebirth" from on high through water and the Spirit, the antecedent condition for entry into the Reign of God to which Jesus makes reference in the dialogue with Nicodemus (John 3:3–8). In like manner, Saint Paul writes that Christians receive "adoption" of children through Christ and his Spirit (Rom. 8:15, 23; Gal. 4:5; Eph. 1:5). After all, in baptism they have received the Holy Spirit, the common Spirit of the Father and the Son, and have become children of God. They have been baptized into the death of Jesus, to rise with him to new life (Rom. 6:1–11; 8:14–24; Gal. 3:25–4:7). Not natural birth, but God's grace in baptism, renders persons children of God through Jesus Christ.

The Pauline and Joannine doctrine of the divine filiation reflects Jesus' own teaching in all of its novelty. Jesus introduces into the Jewish world of his time a radically new comprehension of God. While traditional Hebrew piety placed the accent on God's transcendent majesty and avoided pronouncing his name, YHWH, lest abuses arise, Jesus dares to call God *'Abba.* In the moment of his greatest trial, when God's salvation seems withdrawn from him and he himself is faced with rejection and death, Jesus turns to God in the garden of Gethsemane and says: "Abba, Father, for you all things are possible; remove this cup from me; yet, not what I want, but what you want" (Mark 14:36).

The word *'Abba* is Aramaic, and thus merits special examination on our part. The New Testament was written in Greek; and yet it contains certain Aramaic expressions. Aramaic was the vernacular of the people of Palestine at the time of Jesus. It is very probable that Jesus and his disciples expressed themselves fluently in Aramaic, given the fact that many of the Greek expressions of the New Testament reflect Greek grammar only rather poorly, while they acquire perfect sense once they are recognized as translations from the Aramaic. Besides, some Aramaic words are simply transliterated into Greek. In all probability, these expressions were kept in the original Aramaic because of their importance in the theology and liturgy of the very early Church. Thus, for example, the Aramaic name *Kephas,* which Jesus bestows on Peter, manifests Peter's fundamental role in the primitive Church and indicates more clearly than does the Greek the play on words employed by Jesus. While the Greek proper noun shows its linguistic link with the common noun *petrē,* the identity is not as clear as in Aramaic, where the same word *kephas* means "rock" and is the proper noun or name. Analogously, the retention of the invocation, *Maranatha,* "Our Lord, come!" (1 Cor. 16:22; cf. Rev. 22:20), manifests the Church's burning desire for Christ's return as it is expressed in the liturgy.

Jesus' use of the term *'Abba* was adopted in Christian prayer, as well. "You [Christians] have received a spirit of adoption. When we cry, 'Abba!/Father,' it is that very Spirit bearing witness with our spirit that we are children of God" (Rom. 8:15–16; cf. Gal. 4:6). Literally, *'Abba* is better rendered as "Dad," or "Daddy." It was what young children called their fathers. It could also be used by an older child in token of intimacy and respect. Such was their sense of the transcendence of God that the Hebrews of Palestine did not dare address God as "Daddy." In the Diaspora, outside of Palestine, where the Hebrews tended to assimilate themselves and their thinking to the surrounding culture, in which persons were sometimes addressed as "Father," there were some prayers addressed to YHWH as "Father." Not even in this case, however, did anyone dare address God as "Daddy."

The use of "Father" to designate God was exceedingly rare in Palestine. Modern biblical research has found only one case in which a Palestinian Jew speaks of God as "Father," and even here it is not a matter of an invocation. This text was discovered recently in a fragment of a Qumran manuscript.

Incontestably, Jesus had a unique, intimate relationship with the one he called "Daddy." Because love diffuses itself, Jesus did not keep this relationship for himself. He willed that, thanks to his, others would enter into their own filial relationship with the Father. And so he taught his disciples the Our Father. It is striking that the teaching of this prayer reveals Jesus' unique relationship with the Father and at the same time his desire to communicate that relationship to others. In fact, it is the only case in the Bible in which the expression "Our Father" is pronounced by Jesus himself. Instead, in the other cases in which he was speaking to the disciples, Jesus distinguished only between "my Father" and "your Father" — even, in one passage, using both expressions in the same clause: in John 20:17, in the command given to Mary Magdalen on Easter morning, he says: "Go to my brothers and say to them, 'I am ascending to my Father and your Father, to my God and your God' " (John 20:17). Jesus was well aware that his relationship with the Father could not be reduced to the category of the relationship of his disciples with the Father. In the moment when he taught them to pray the Our Father, he was the intermediary of their relationship with God. Of course, Jesus called God "Father" only when instructing the disciples. Nonbelievers had not been introduced into the intimacy with God that Jesus offered the believing disciples. As Saint Paul grasped, one must have received the Spirit of Jesus in order to be able to cry, "Abba / Father" (Rom. 8:15). Ultimately, the entire Christian life is a sharing of the life of Jesus Christ, the only Son of God.

Consequences of Being Children of God

Election to the filiation of God does not authorize the Christian to be triumphalistic, or to look down on those who have not reached faith. No believer can boast before God, inasmuch as his or her salvation is only a divine gift (1 Cor. 1:26–31). "I have come to call not the righteous but sinners" (Mark 2:17). Of course, in this Jesus only manifests the same attitude of love that characterizes his Father. Addressing the disciples, Jesus describes the Father's behavior with regard to sinners in terms not simply of extreme fairness, but of patience and love:

> You have heard that it was said, "You shall love your neighbor and hate your enemy." But I say to you, Love your enemies and pray for those who persecute you, so that you may be children of your Father in heaven; for he makes his sun rise on the evil and on the good, and sends rain on the righteous and on the unrighteous. For if you love those who love you, what reward do you have? Do not even the tax collectors do the same? And if you greet only your brothers and sisters, what more are you doing than others? Do not even the Gentiles do the same? Be perfect, therefore, as your heavenly Father is perfect. (Matt. 5:43–48)

Rather than regarding his disciples as an elite to be served, Jesus asks them to serve, and to extend to other persons the filial relationship in which they have been made sharers (Matt. 20:20–28): " ... Baptizing them in the name of the Father and of the Son and of the Holy Spirit" (Matt. 28:19). Furthermore, Christians may not cling to their condition of being God's children as a permanent, static possession. It is a dynamic reality, which must be developed on the foundations with which it is endowed. Precisely as the Reign of God is a reality both present and future, which reflects the tension between the indicative of God's love and the imperative of the response to this love, so also the condition of being children of God granted to men and

women is directed toward the future. Saint Paul wrote to the
Christians of Rome:

> You did not receive a spirit of slavery to fall back into
> fear, but you have received a spirit of adoption. When
> we cry, "Abba / Father!" it is that very Spirit bearing wit-
> ness with our spirit that we are children of God, and if
> children, then heirs, heirs of God and joint heirs with
> Christ — if, in fact, we suffer with him so that we may
> also be glorified with him. (Rom. 8:15–17)

While the spirit of adoption is genuinely bestowed, allowing
believers to pray, that Spirit is not their guarantee of unconditional salvation. They must suffer with Christ in order to share
his glory. In other words, their faithfulness must still pass the
test. Owing to this future uncertainty, in the verses immediately
following Paul presents the condition of being children of God
as a gift still to be revealed and bestowed:

> I consider that the sufferings of this present time are not
> worth comparing with the glory about to be revealed
> to us. For the creation waits with eager longing for the
> revealing of the children of God; for the creation was
> subjected to futility, not of its own will but by the will
> of the one who subjected it, in hope that the creation it-
> self will be set free from its bondage to decay and will
> obtain the freedom of the glory of the children of God.
> We know that the whole creation has been groaning in
> labor pains until now; and not only the creation, but we
> ourselves, who have the first fruits of the Spirit, groan in-
> wardly while we wait for adoption, the redemption of our
> bodies. (Rom. 8:18–23)

The Christian life still has room for growth in grace. The
Church is invited to grow "to maturity, to the measure of the
full stature of Christ" (Eph. 4:13; cf. 1:22–23; 4:11–16; Col.
1:18–20). Precisely as Jesus had commanded his disciples to be
perfect as their Father in heaven is perfect, thus encouraging

them to a continuous growth in the mystery of love, so also
Saint Paul exhorted Christians to grow continuously as children of God to the very fullness of Christ. Indeed, in his own
life, the Apostle, with his sufferings, generated the believers of
Galatia to faith, in order that Christ might be formed in them
(Gal. 4:13–14). Correspondingly, he saw his own sufferings as
a sharing of the sufferings of Christ, furnishing the basis for
a hope to be conformed to Christ's death in such a way as to
attain the resurrection from the dead (Phil. 3:10–11).

There is a certain parallelism between the theology of the
image and that of the filiation of God. Both presuppose a
relationship with God that includes the tension between the
present and the future in which the present gift furnishes
the foundation for its future complement. But there is also a
marked difference. The image of God comes from creation,
and, while it is given in view of Christ, it must be completed
through an acceptance of the newness of Christ in faith and
love. The divine filiation, on the other hand, implies from the
outset a relationship with Christ in faith and love. Faith emphasizes the continuity between creation and salvation; love
stresses the growth of the beginnings of redemption to their
very completion in Christ. The breach in salvation history characterizes all historical religions. Something new has happened
in time that was not present in creation, and that something
is decisive for the eternal destiny of the human being. Because salvation embraces the human being's relationship with
God, the element of novelty in the history of salvation must
reach God.

Chapter 4

God the Father of Mercy

Revelation of the Name of God, Infinite Mercy

"Mercy is ... proper to God"

Saint Thomas Aquinas's assertion in his *Summa Theologiae* is crisp: "Mercy is accounted as being proper to God: and therein His omnipotence is declared to be chiefly manifested" (*ST* IIa-IIae, q. 30, a. 4, c.). The great medieval theologian is underscoring the fact that mercy does not express only an exterior attitude on God's part, let alone one of weakness. On the contrary, mercy is a sovereign attribute of omnipotence. Besides being revealed as transcendent, holy, eternal, and omnipotent, God is revealed as merciful as well: "Father, you show your almighty power in your mercy and forgiveness." Thus we pray in the Opening Prayer of the Twenty-Sixth Sunday of Ordinary Time (B). Forgiveness and mercy are actually a sovereign act of the omnipotence of God.

All of this corresponds to the revelation of the name and reality of God in the Old Testament itself. Indeed, God is first manifested to Moses as "I am who I am" (Exod. 32:14), that is, as provident and almighty presence. This first revelation of the name is followed by a second, which completes it. Still on Sinai, and passing before Moses, the Lord proclaims:

> The Lord, the Lord,
> a God merciful and gracious,
> slow to anger,
> and abounding in steadfast love and faithfulness,
> keeping steadfast love for the thousandth generation,
> forgiving iniquity and transgression and sin.
>
> (Exod. 34:6–7)

43

Besides being almighty, God is also merciful. Indeed, this will be the divine name to be evoked most frequently in the history of the chosen people.

"The Lord is gracious and merciful"

The words expressing the manifold content of mercy in all languages are many: compassion, pity, clemency, charity, forgiveness, indulgence, benevolence, benignity, meekness. Further, in the Old Testament, God's mercy is not expressed in words alone — as, for example, *hesed* (faithfulness) or *rahamim,* love (plural of *rehem:* the maternal bosom) — but also in symbols, images, and God's merciful and loving attitudes toward all creatures, especially toward the chosen people. In songs of prayer, invocation, and thanksgiving, the Lord is celebrated as "gracious and merciful" (Ps. 111:4), and the divine name, which is mercy and goodness, is exalted:

> The Lord is gracious and merciful,
> slow to anger and abounding in steadfast love.
> The Lord is good to all,
> and his compassion is over all that he has made.
> (Ps. 145:8–9)

The theme of the Lord's goodness and mercy is frequently evoked, with slight variations:

> But you, O Lord, are a God merciful and gracious,
> slow to anger and abounding in steadfast love and
>   faithfulness.
> Turn to me and be gracious to me;
> give your strength to your servant;
> save the child of your serving girl.
> Show me a sign of your favor
> so that those who hate me may see it and be put to
>   shame,
> because you, Lord, have helped me and comforted me.
> (Ps. 86:15–17)

The Lord is merciful and gracious
slow to anger and abounding in steadfast love.

(Ps. 103:8)

The "great mercies of the Lord" (cf. Ps. 119:156) are exalted
by the Psalmist with a vividness and variety of images:

As the heavens are high above the earth,
so great is his steadfast love toward those who fear him;
as far as the east is from the west,
so far he removes our transgressions from us.
As a father has compassion for his children,
so the Lord has compassion for those who fear him.

(Ps. 103:11–13)

The Lord's goodness, manifested in concrete actions of forgiveness, of healing, of assistance, is like a "crown" on the head of
the human being. For the Lord is the one

who forgives all your iniquity,
who heals all your diseases,
who redeems your life from the Pit,
who crowns you with steadfast love and mercy.

(Ps. 103:3–4)

The Lord upholds all who are falling,
and raises up all who are bowed down.

(Ps. 145:14)

The Lord sets the prisoners free;
the Lord opens the eyes of the blind.
The Lord lifts up those who are bowed down;
the Lord loves the righteous.
The Lord watches over the strangers;
he upholds the orphan and the widow
but the way of the wicked he brings to ruin.

(Ps. 146:7–9)

> He heals the brokenhearted,
> and binds up their wounds. . . .
> The Lord lifts up the downtrodden;
> he casts the wicked to the ground.
>   (Ps. 147:3–6)

In virtue of this protection and guidance, the Lord is compared to the good shepherd who diligently, solicitously, leads his flock to fresh and abundant pastures:

> The Lord is my shepherd, I shall not want.
> He makes me lie down in green pastures;
> he leads me beside still waters;
> he restores my soul.
> He leads me in right paths
> for his name's sake.

> Even though I walk through the darkest valley,
> I fear no evil;
> for you are with me; . . .

> Surely goodness and mercy shall follow me
> all the days of my life,
> and I shall dwell in the house of the Lord
> my whole life long. (Ps. 23:1–6)

Thus, the psalmist's cry of joy comes as no surprise:

> Happy are the people whose God is the Lord.
>   (Ps. 144:15)

> Bless the Lord, O my soul,
> and do not forget all his benefits. (Ps. 103:2)

"The eye of the Lord is on those who fear him"

Again, the image of the watchful eye, symbol of omniscience, watchfulness, and protective omnipresence, becomes the expression of the divine goodness and mercy:

> Truly the eye of the Lord is on those who fear him,
> on those who hope in his steadfast love,
> to deliver their soul from death,
> and to keep them alive in famine. (Ps. 33:18–19)

> His eyes behold, his gaze examines humankind.
> The Lord tests the righteous and the wicked,
> and his soul hates the lover of violence. (Ps. 11:4–5)

Despite the people's infidelities and apostasies, God remains faithful to the divine promise. Thus, the Lord expresses the divine mercy through the mouth of the prophet Ezekiel: "Nevertheless my eye spared them, and I did not destroy them or make an end of them in the wilderness" (Ezek. 20:17). Protected by the merciful eye of the Lord, human beings, in their turn, turn their gaze toward the Lord to invoke protection and salvation. We have an exchange of glance between child and parent:

> My eyes are ever toward the Lord,
> for he will pluck my feet out of the net.

> Turn to me and be gracious to me,
> for I am lonely and afflicted. (Ps. 25:15–16)

> But my eyes are turned toward you, O God, my Lord;
> in you I seek refuge; do not leave me defenseless.
> (Ps. 141:8)

> The eyes of all look to you,
> and you give them their food in due season.
> (Ps. 145:15)

In virtue of God's readiness to assist, forgive, and have mercy, tirelessly the psalmist sings the mercy of God as everlasting:

> I give thanks to you, O Lord my God, with my whole
> heart,
> and I will glorify your name forever.

For great is your steadfast love toward me;
you have delivered my soul from the depths of Sheol.
                                        (Ps. 86:12–13)

O give thanks to the Lord, for he is good;
his steadfast love endures forever!
Let Israel say,
"His steadfast love endures forever."
Let the house of Aaron say,
"His steadfast love endures forever."
Let those who fear the Lord say,
"His steadfast love endures forever."
O give thanks to the Lord, for he is good,
for his steadfast love endures forever.
                                        (Ps. 118:1–4, 29)

An entire psalm, Psalm 136, rereads God's work in creation, the election, and the protection of the people in the light of the divine mercy and goodness, which thus becomes the refrain of each acclamation:

O give thanks to the Lord, for he is good,
for his steadfast love endures forever;...
for his steadfast love endures forever. (Ps. 136:1–26)

Those who believe in the Lord find themselves utterly immersed in God's parental embrace, and God becomes their refuge:

You hem me in, behind and before,
and lay your hand upon me. (Ps. 139:5)

You are a hiding place for me;
you preserve me from trouble;
you surround me with glad cries of deliverance.
                                        (Ps. 32:7)

If my father and mother forsake me,
the Lord will take me up. (Ps. 27:10)

"As a mother comforts her child, so will I comfort you"

The Lord's sweet, consoling presence in the Old Testament is also expressed in images of motherly tenderness:

> I have calmed and quieted my soul,
> like a weaned child with its mother;
> my soul is like the weaned child that is with me.
> (Ps. 131:2)

> Can a woman forget her nursing child,
> or show no compassion for the child of her womb?
> Even these may forget,
> yet I will not forget you. (Isa. 49:15)

> As a mother comforts her child,
> so will I comfort you. (Isa. 66:13)

Hosea, too, likens God's behavior toward the people to that of an affectionate parent toward a little child:

> When Israel was a child, I loved him,
> and out of Egypt I called my son. . . .
> It was I who taught Ephraim to walk,
> I took them up in my arms;
> but they did not know that I healed them.
> I led them with cords of human kindness,
> with bands of love.
> I was to them like those
> who lift infants to their cheeks,
> I bent down to them and fed them. . . .
> My heart recoils within me,
> my compassion grows warm and tender.
> (Hos. 11:1–8)

While God is spoken of elsewhere as a father, the images used by the prophet are those typical of a solicitous mother, caring for her smallest children. She teaches them to walk by holding their hand, she lifts them to kiss them on the cheek, she bends down to feed them. God uses the same pedagogy of love toward the people as any mother practices with her children.

For Isaiah, it is as the people had been generated and nourished by God from the maternal womb:

Listen to me, O house of Jacob,
all the remnant of the house of Israel,
who have been borne by me from your birth,
carried from the womb. (Isa. 46:3)

And again:

Thus says the Lord who made you,
who formed you in the womb and will help you.
                                                        (Isa. 44:2)

Thus says the Lord, your Redeemer,
who formed you in the womb. (Isa. 44:24)

While the maternal womb spoken of in these passages is that of earthly mothers, the declarations express God's continuous providence and mercy toward creatures. Thus the psalmist says:

Upon you I have leaned from my birth;
it was you who took me from my mother's womb.
                                                        (Ps. 71:6)

It was you who formed my inward parts;
you knit me together in my mother's womb. (Ps. 139:13)

Using a somewhat different image, rather than that of a mother, the psalms compare God to a nursemaid, who tenderly lays a newborn on its mother's breast:

On you I was cast from my birth,
and since my mother bore me you have been my God.
                                                        (Ps. 22:10)

In the Bible, the words *rahamim* ("entrails," "mercy") and *rahum* ("merciful") are applied to God. They are related to *rehem*, "motherly bosom" — the place of care, defense, and growth of life in its first beginnings. These words express all but a physical mercy on the part of God, who is a love with "bowels of mercy," as if God had inward parts that wrenched with compassion at the sight of creatures' suffering, a profound, spontaneous, inward love, a love charged with the tenderness, sympathy, compassion, indulgence, and forgiveness that bind a mother to her children (cf., e.g., Isa. 49:15, above, and Exod. 34:6–7).

Besides being expressed in anthropomorphic symbols and metaphors, the notion of the divine mercy is also clothed in symbols inspired by nature. God is called the sun (Ps. 84:11), a rock (Deut. 32:15), fire (Deut. 4:24). The divine protection is compared to an eagle's for her eaglets:

> As an eagle stirs up its nest,
> and hovers over its young,
> as it spreads its wings, takes them up,
> and bears them aloft on its pinions,
> the Lord alone guided him. (Deut. 32:11–12)

This may be the origin of the expression used in certain psalms: "In the shadow of your wings I will take refuge" (Ps. 57:1; cf. 17:8; 36:7; 61:4; 63:7; 91:4; cf. also Exod. 19:4; Ruth 2:12).

Further, God is referred to — perhaps not as frequently as we might expect — now as Father of the people (cf., for example, Exod. 4:22–23; Deut. 1:31; 14:1; 32:5–6; Isa. 63:16; 64:7), now as faithful and loving spouse (cf., for example, Isa. 5:1–7; Ezek. 16; 23). And as father and spouse (Isa. 62:4–5; Hos. 2:18, 21–22) he has motherly feelings of tenderness, bounty, and mercy.

As we have emphasized above, the Old Testament does not devote a great deal of relevancy to the name of God as "Father," especially in the first books of the Bible. The reason for this is the concern of the sacred writers to maintain the originality of the monotheistic conceptualization, which, unlike the Canaanite culture, does not permit bonds of propagation between the divinity and the people. The God of Israel is not that Father-God who is the mythical biological progenitor of the people. In the Old Testament, the title "Father," when referring to God, expresses primarily God's creative power, protection, authority, and maintenance of life. It is a powerful allusion to the goodness, at once fatherly and motherly, that God as provident Creator demonstrates vis-à-vis the people in need.

Jesus, Incarnation and Revelation of the Father's Mercy

If the Old Testament expresses the divine mercy in a multiplicity of expressions, attitudes, and comparisons, the New Testament concentrates the manifestation of God's mercy in the person and work of Jesus Christ: "Long ago God spoke to our ancestors in many and various ways by the prophets, but in these last days he has spoken to us by a Son" (Heb. 1:1–2). John Paul II says: "Christ bestows a definitive signification on the whole of the Old Testament tradition of the divine mercy. Not only does he speak of it, and explain it in parables, but, especially, he himself incarnates and personifies it. He himself is, in a certain sense, mercy" (*DM*, no. 2). The Incarnation of the Word is not only a work of the charity of God (cf. John 3:16), but also the supreme revelation of the divine mercy become a person.

Jesus Christ, the "Only-begotten Son, who is in the bosom of the Father" (cf. John 1:18), the visible "image of the invisible God" (Col. 1:15), is in his person, in his words, in his actions, and in his attitudes the merciful face of a Father "rich in mercy" (Eph. 2:4). His event, from his birth to his resurrection, is the most complete account of the mercy of the God who is Trinity. He sees, speaks, acts, heals, moved by pity and mercy toward the numberless needy, disinherited, and sick of every kind and every place, who hasten to him: the blind, the crippled, paralytics, sinners, the poor, children, women, foreigners, the possessed, lepers, enemies. To John's disciples, who asked him whether he was the Messiah, he responded with a reference to the works of mercy: "The blind receive their sight, the lame walk, the lepers are cleansed, the deaf hear, the dead are raised, the poor have good news brought to them" (Luke 7:22). Jesus' parables of mercy, recounted in order to proclaim the divine bounty, are most vivid: the sheep lost and found again, the coin lost and recovered, the prodigal child received into the wide-open arms of a good, compassionate parent (Luke 15).

In the Gospel of Saint Matthew, responding to the Pharisees' criticisms, Jesus twice refers to an incisive assertion of the prophet Hosea: "I desire steadfast love and not sacrifice" (Hos. 6:6). The first time, having called the tax collector Matthew to follow him, he tells the Pharisees, "Go and learn what this means, 'I desire mercy, not sacrifice' " (Matt. 9:13). The second time, once more in response to the Pharisees, who were criticizing the disciples for having plucked heads of grain on the Sabbath because they were hungry, he quotes the same line: "If you had known what this means, 'I desire mercy and not sacrifice,' you would not have condemned the guiltless" (Matt. 12:7).

The Paschal mystery of Jesus' death and resurrection is the pinnacle of the revelation of the divine mercy: it is the gift of the Son to the merciful Father in the embrace of love of the Holy Spirit. It is out of love that the Father sends the Son into the world. It is out of love that Christ offers himself to the Father for the redemption of sinful humanity: "No one has greater love than this, to lay down one's life for one's friends" (John 15:13). It is out of love that the risen Christ bestows the Holy Spirit on his Church: "Receive the Holy Spirit. If you forgive the sins of any, they are forgiven them; if you retain the sins of any, they are retained" (John 20:22–23). The final act of the risen Christ was to bestow upon his disciples the divine power to forgive sins. To believe in God is to believe in mercy, and "the Paschal Christ is the definitive incarnation of mercy, its living sign (*vivens signum*) at once one of salvation history and eschatological" (*DM*, no. 8).

The entire existence of Jesus, incarnate Son of God, was so steeped in goodness and mercy that Saint John, the truthful witness (cf. 3 John 12), defines God in one word: *agapē* (love, charity: 1 John 4:8, 16). At last the Old Testament revelation of the name of God — God is "the one who is" (cf. Exod. 3:14) — receives its complement: God is "the one who is gracious and merciful" (cf. Exod. 34:6). "God is love, and those who abide in love abide in God, and God abides in them" (1 John 4:16).

If love is the nature of God, then the creature, too, the image most like unto God, is called to become mercy. "Be merciful, just as your Father is merciful" (Luke 6:36). That is, it is a matter of acquiring the perfection of the charity of the Father: "Be perfect, therefore, as your heavenly Father is perfect" (Matt. 5:48), the "God and Father of our Lord Jesus Christ, the Father of mercies and the God of all consolation, who consoles us in all our affliction, so that we may be able to console those who are in any affliction with the consolation with which we ourselves are consoled by God" (2 Cor. 1:3–4). This is what Jesus has done, becoming "a merciful and faithful high priest in the service of God, to make a sacrifice of atonement for the sins of the people" (Heb. 2:17). Hence the mercy and the beatitude of the disciple of Christ: "Blessed are the merciful, for they will receive mercy" (Matt. 5:7).

Parable of Mercy

The mystery of God "recounted" by Jesus (cf. John 1:18) is the mystery of God the Father: "I have made your name known to those whom you gave me from the world" (John 17:6). It is especially the Gospel of John that is the gospel of the revelation of the name of God, as Father, but also as Son and Holy Spirit, as well as God in the Trinitarian communion. In the New Testament, God, the Father of Jesus Christ (203 times) and the Father of believers (53 times), is a most loving and compassionate Father, like the father of the familiar parable in Luke 15:11–32.

It is a memorable page of God's goodness, as reflected in the compassion and tenderness of an earthly father. It consists of a drama in two acts. The first act speaks of human misery — in the case before us, that of the flight of the younger son and the mean-spiritedness of the older. The second act is the story of the free, limitless mercy of God, who forgives the younger son and understands the older. Misery and mercy. Not crime and punishment, but crime and mercy.

In this parable, the younger son is presented as dissatisfied and distressed. He wishes to change his life, to leave it. And indeed he leaves his father's house, to experience independence, love, freedom, and self-realization. It is a photograph of a common phenomenon of every human existence. The moment arrives when we feel weary, prisoners of a given situation, and we wish a change. There are times when we feel surrounded only by indifference and solitude. Actually we are not. A loving Father is still waiting. A return to the Father's house is still an option. God is the hope of the anguished. Trust in life is restored to the dissatisfied children of God. God embraces them. God is our hope.

But we are God's hope, as well. God never despairs of our conversion and return. While it is true that, in this parable, hope identifies God, it is likewise true that, in the same parable, it identifies the new human being of the New Testament: a person who, when in crisis and danger, is assisted and saved, not judged and condemned.

The parable consists of twenty verses, with three personages: the rebellious, impatient younger son, the lover of adventure; the merciful father, patient and limitlessly munificent; and the older son, industrious and faithful, but also mean, jealous, and selfish.

The key personage of the parable is obviously the father, who hopes against hope for the return of his lost child. He represents God our Father, who never discriminates among the children of God and never tires of awaiting the return of wandering children. For Jesus tells us that the heavenly Father "makes his sun rise on the evil and on the good, and sends rain on the righteous and on the unrighteous" (Matt. 5:45).

This two-thousand-year-old parable touches the hearts of all, giving them back their deepest, most tender sentiments, and bringing them from selfishness to generosity, from meanness to sharing. It is the parable — as Charles Péguy puts it — that "has remained driven into the heart of the impious as a nail of tenderness." We can resist truth, we can even resist beauty; but we surrender to tenderness, to forgiving, generous welcome, to this wonderful blossom of gratuitous love.

Rainer Maria Rilke saw in the parable of the prodigal son the drama of persons who refuse to be loved. Leaving the house of the Father, they leave the house of love — to which, nevertheless, they must return, since every heart, sooner or later, returns to the source of charity.

God the Father, in this parable, has the afflicted mien of one suffering on account of the prodigal son, the lost sheep, the traveler set upon by violent persons and left to die by the roadside. It is the parable in which we see the depth of the merciful heart of God, but also the depth of the heart of God's children, who slam behind them the doors of the parental home. It is the story not of one prodigal son, but of two prodigal siblings: the first flees the Father, the second refuses the Father's compassion and forgiveness. Paradoxically, at the conclusion of the parable, the sinful son becomes the example to imitate, while the "faithful" son becomes the example to avoid. The first becomes lovable, the second detestable. And yet, God still loves both. He loves the prodigal hoping for his return, he loves the older son hoping for conversion of heart as well. God's occupation is to love. Only God can love in this fashion, because only God is defined as "love" (1 John 4:8, 16).

On this point, the Christianity of the first centuries wrought a towering accomplishment of inculturation of the faith, significantly purifying currents of Greco-Latin thought from deeply anti-Christian conceptions. Plato, Aristotle, and, especially, the Stoics, tended to regard mercy, pity, and compassion as useless sentimentalism. Mercy for Aristotle was not a virtue, but a weakness of the elderly and children. For the Stoics, it was a mental aberration. The Fathers of the Church opposed this view, embracing the points of departure offered by, for example, Cicero, who rejected the Stoic conception of mercy as absurd, and for whom mercy was an index of wisdom, morality, and goodness.

God's Eyes of Mercy

It would not be incorrect to assert that, today, while there are theologies of hope, or theologies of liberation, or theologies of inculturation, there is no theology of mercy. The explanation is perhaps to be sought in a certain contemporary mentality that "seems to oppose the God of mercy, and furthermore tends to marginalize the very idea of mercy from life, and distract the human heart from it" (*DM*, no. 2).

Nonetheless, there have been some theologians to have plumbed the theme of mercy with originality. For example, in the 1950s theologian Reginald Garrigou-Lagrange wrote: "In the psalms, three words always appear together: the misery of the human being, who calls upon the mercy of God, which redounds to the divine glory." And he went on: "The divine mercy is like the root and principle of all of the works of God; it penetrates them with its power, and dominates them. As primordial font of all of the gifts, it is mercy that is most influential. Thus, it surpasses even justice, which comes only in second place and is subordinate to mercy." The decisive deed of the Father, then, is mercy. In this is hidden the mystery of the divine love, which goes so far as even to forgive. Forgiveness calls all to a new existence: that of the authentic children of God.

Chapter 5

Gift of Forgiveness

The death and resurrection of Jesus Christ are the unshakable foundation of the Christian faith. The Paschal mystery is neither a philosophical theory, nor an experience within reach of all persons, nor the projection of human hopes for a better existence. It is a fact attested by witnesses chosen by God, prepared for their task by the invitation to share Jesus' life and ministry (Acts 1:8, 21–22; 10:39–42; 13:31). Our sole route of access to this historical fact is precisely the testimony of those who have proclaimed the good news of salvation, proclaiming the love that has defeated sin and death in the death and resurrection of Jesus Christ. The revelation and salvation effected by this mystery have continuous need of the mediation of history. While all theological reflection is linked to it as God's full revelation to human beings, and consequently is to be judged by its conformity with that revelation, the latter contains a human intelligibility that can be expressed in words. After all, not only was Jesus "handed over to death for our trespasses," but he was "raised for our justification," as well (Rom. 4:25). Indeed, in order to prevent the definitive revelation on the cross and in the resurrection from going for naught, God had to include in the resurrection event some comprehension of it on the part of the disciples. These had been called to accept, in freedom, the risen Jesus, and to preach his death and resurrection for the faith of others.

Scripture testifies to the primacy of the resurrection. Except for his Virgin Mother, all of the disciples had betrayed, denied, and abandoned him. They had expected a glorious Messianic kingdom, in which they would have had enjoyed positions of authority, lording it over others (Mark 10:35–45).

58

Repeatedly, Jesus had told them that "the Son of Man came not to be served but to serve, and to give his life a ransom for many" (Mark 10:45). And yet the delusion of the expectation of grandeur prevented the disciples from identifying the suffering Son of Man with Jesus, whom Peter had recognized as the Messiah so long awaited, destined to establish God's Reign of justice on earth (cf. Mark 8:27–33). As the Transfiguration account shows, Peter's desire was to keep the glory in "dwellings" or tents without reaching the cross. But the voice of the Father brought him back to the reality of the cross with the command, "Listen to him!" (Mark 9:2–13; see also Mark 8:34–9:1; Luke 9:31–32). The cross took the disciples and their too human hopes by surprise. The risen Christ appears to persons of disillusioned hopes, to fearful persons without faith, to traitors without love, calling them to faith.

Gospel Call to Repentance

The exordium of Mark's Gospel summarizes Jesus' message: "The time is fulfilled, and the kingdom of God has come near; repent, and believe in the good news" (Mark 1:15). It is worth noticing that, in the original text, the Greek verbs for "to fulfill" and "to be near" are in the perfect tense. This tense does not indicate simply a past action, but a past action that has consequences in the present. For instance, the Greek perfect in the phrase, "I have hit him in the eye," would imply the consequence of this action: a black eye. The result of the fulfillment of the time and the approach of the Kingdom of God is given in the crisp command, "Repent, and believe in the good news." With this tension between the indicative and the imperative, Jesus meant that God's initiative, suddenly appearing in history, was already winning a response from human freedom, in terms of repentance and faith. The primacy of the divine intervention does not, then, cancel the free choice of the person, but invites that person to act.

The Greek word usually translated as "repent," here used in

the imperative (*metanoiete*), literally means "change ideas," or
"change your hearts." Jesus was inviting persons to move in
a new direction, to change their lives radically. After all, any
change of ideas or hearts must be manifested in concrete de-
cisions, in "works worthy of conversion" (cf. Luke 3:8). Jesus
repeatedly asked conversion of his hearers (Matt. 11:20–21;
12:41; Luke 13:3, 5; 15:7–10). This change in the direction
of their lives would be bound up with faith: "Believe in the
Gospel." The object of faith was constituted now by Jesus,
now by his words (Mark 8:38; John 2:11, 22–23; 3:15, 18;
4:39, 41, 50), inasmuch as a person is manifested in words,
and words reveal the person. The Word was known through
his words, even though his full personal reality could not be
contained completely in words (John 21:25). Although the
burden of his message was the Reign of God, there was no sep-
aration between Jesus and his message. In him, the only sinless
one, God's sign of love was embodied and manifested. He was
the fulcrum of conversion, the cornerstone of authenticity: "Do
not let your hearts be troubled. Believe in God, believe also in
me.... No one comes to the Father except through me" (John
14:1–6).

Drama of Sin

Justice of God

The Catholic understanding of original sin, based on the
teaching of Genesis and of Saint Paul, absolves God of all
responsibility for evil in the world. God is just and must be
regarded as just in every work and deed. This explanation,
however, seems to contrast with the portrait of a God who
somehow condemns to the "punishment" of suffering all persons after Adam even before they commit a personal sin. Can
such a God be just?

Of course, we find ourselves before a real dilemma. Sins
have consequences, and we cannot isolate human beings from

one another without destroying their nature. After all, persons find themselves in a natural solidarity with one another by birth. All are touched by the sins of others, especially by the sins of their parents. Consequently, infants are inevitably condemned from their very birth. A like scenario seems very unjust to the modern human being.

In any case, however, the rejection of God solves no problems. Unless there is a life after death, with an all-knowing, all-powerful God rendering justice to each according to his or her deserts, justice would become a mere word without content: if this world is the way it is, and justice cannot be found in it, then justice nowhere exists. The rejection of God on the part of modern atheism has made no progress against the human being's dilemma: it has only made it uncontrollable. Without God, there is no hope of justice for a world steeped in injustice and the absence of love. Not even the best judges can impose law upon earth. The concept of justice tends to change in function of the notions of human beings, who form their opinions on the basis of offenses directly experienced by themselves. When a transgression is committed and a penalty imposed, the penalty may be perceived by the party upon whom it is imposed not as justice, but as vengeance, and a new cry for punishment arises.

In his *Orestes,* Greek tragedian Aeschylus describes the condition of the human being as an unstoppable chain of transgression, punishment, and reprisal. It ravages the house of Atreus through successive generations, because the reestablishment of right by one party is felt as injustice by the other. The cycle of punishments seemed infinite. Each party, in its initiatives of punishment, claimed that this was justice, and interpreted the action of the other as lawless criminality. There was no escape from the dilemma of conflictive claims until a divine power, the goddess Athena, was introduced by Aeschylus to establish the tribunal of the Areopagus at Athens. The duty of this tribunal was to decide among the contradictory claims that threatened to rend the fabric of Athenian society.

Declaring absolution in equally valid accusatory and defense arguments, the goddess succeeded in establishing a kind of peace for the house of Atreus. The subsequent history of Athens, however, showed that any tribunal confided to human judges would fall prey to divisions and conflicts. Advocates justified their evaluation of the cases in function of the need of their clients. When the resemblance of their position to law and precedents was advantageous for their client, they stressed the analogy. When they had need of the opposite, they underscored how different the present case ought to seem from the intent of the law and from precedents. Ultimately the people lost confidence in these sophistical manipulations of justice. Persons frequently solicit solidarity when they have no other recourse, and then, when circumstances have changed, reverse their position, emphasizing their autonomy, so that many, like Plato, despaired of finding a perfect human justice on this earth. Aeschylus had grasped the need for a merciful divine intervention in order to solve the dilemmas of justice, but the merely human court of the Areopagus was not equal to a divine task. Someone had to break the chain of transgression that seeks punishment and offense that seeks revenge.

Intervention of God

The human being's sense of justice is not the measure of its reality. God is not bound by a notion of justice such as expressed in the proverbial "tit for tat," as if human beings and God were equals under a superior notion of justice. There is no norm of justice apart from or above God. God is just by nature, and the divine justice, Scripture teaches, is justifying: that is, God loves sinners and justifies them gratuitously. Inasmuch as God is love, and justice is identical with God, justice must be understood in terms of God's love.

God is not bound by the present order of creation. But, although there was therefore no obligation on God's part to save human beings from their sins, the divine love chose to snatch them indeed from the devastating chain of sin. Even if the human being has rejected this love, God has never rejected the human being. Saint Irenaeus notes that, even in expelling Adam from the earthly paradise, God showed the divine love by replacing the coarse fig leaves that scratched human flesh with softer, protective garments fashioned from animal skins (Gen. 3:21). Irenaeus regarded the new distance from the tree of life (Gen. 3:22–24), too, as a blessing, "lest the human being remain forever a transgressor, ... and evil be without end or healing" (*Adversus Haereses*, 3, 23, 5–6; *PG* 7, 963A–964A). Of course, a still greater sign of God's love was the promise to send someone of the descendancy of Eve, who would crush the serpent's head (Gen. 3:15). This promise looked ahead to the sole Savior of humanity, Jesus Christ.

Jesus Christ became sin for love of us. As Saint Paul writes: "We entreat you on behalf of Christ, be reconciled to God. For our sake he made him to be sin who knew no sin, so that in him we might become the righteousness of God" (2 Cor. 5:20–21). Thus the furthest poles became unified: the holiest love, which is God, was joined to sinful humanity: Jesus entered freely into the world to die for us. It is the Apostle, once more, who declares:

> For while we were still weak, at the right time Christ died for the ungodly. Indeed, rarely will anyone die for a righteous person — although perhaps for a good person someone might actually dare to die. But God proves his love for us in that while we still were sinners Christ died for us. Much more surely then, now that we have been justified by his blood, will we be saved through him from the wrath of God. (Rom. 5:6–9)

Chapter 6

Salvation, Reconciliation, and Penance

As we have seen in the preceding chapter, once they had sinned, human beings could not of themselves have attained to any security with regard to love and the meaning of their lives. God had to intervene with the incarnation of the divine Son in order to guarantee the human being that love is actually stronger than sin. In his resurrection, Christ revealed the love that triumphs over death. The Word of God has pronounced a word of love understandable by all. But this word creates what it proclaims. The prophet Isaiah describes the efficacity of the Word of God:

> For as the rain and snow come down from heaven,
> and do not return there until they have watered the earth,
> making it bring forth and sprout,
> giving seed to the sower and bread to the eater,
> so shall my word be that goes out from my mouth;
> it shall not return to me empty,
> but it shall accomplish that which I purpose.
>
> (Isa. 55:10–11)

Once the word of God is addressed to them, human beings are under constraint. They must respond. Either love generates love, or it is the occasion of a rejection. Jesus' proclamation of the Reign of God, realized in his person, is an invitation and a challenge for the human being.

Accepting Jesus means sharing his life and following him to the cross — that is, loving him to the death.

To be united in love to Jesus means to live by his love — to share his life and love, which has conquered sin and death: "It

64

is no longer I who live, but it is Christ who lives in me. And the life I now live in the flesh I live by faith in the Son of God, who loved me and gave himself for me" (Gal. 2:20).

The Sacrament of Penance

Baptism is a complete consecration to God, who has bestowed upon human beings the gift of the divine self. Unfortunately, believers sin after baptism. This fact is frequently attested in the New Testament. Besides predicting the tribulations of the end of the ages, and the sudden deception of many at the hands of false prophets (Mark 13:5–6, 21–22), Jesus cites a sinful conduct among the "brothers and sisters." As long as the siblings are divided, their relationship with God is disturbed: "So when you are offering your gift at the altar, if you remember that your brother or sister has something against you, leave your gift there before the altar and go; first be reconciled to your brother or sister, and then come and offer your gift" (Matt. 5:23–24). The import of reconciliation is not limited to reparation of offenses on the part of individuals. The community of the Church is concerned with the process of reconciliation when the siblings have failed to reach agreement:

> If another member of the church sins against you, go and point out the fault when the two of you are alone. If the member listens to you, you have regained that one. But if you are not listened to, take one or two others along with you, so that every word may be confirmed by the evidence of two or three witnesses. If the member refuses to listen to them, tell it to the church; and if the offender refuses to listen even to the church, let such a one be to you as a Gentile and a tax collector. Truly I tell you, whatever you bind on earth will be bound in heaven, and whatever you loose on earth will be loosed in heaven. (Matt. 18:15–18; cf. 16:19)

Even the primitive Church, as we see, was torn by the sins of its members. The apostolic letters are filled with exhortations to avoid sin, to practice virtue, and to preserve the faith against false teachers. The Book of Revelation presents a collection of letters addressed to various churches demanding that they do penance (Rev. 2:1–3:22). Even the heads of local churches could sin (3 John 9–12), and Saint Paul recalls having reproved Peter for not living in conformity with the Gospel by having refused to take meals with non-Jewish Christians who did not follow the Mosaic law (Gal. 2:11–21). Analogously, Paul feared to find, upon returning to Corinth, "quarreling, jealousy, anger, selfishness, slander, gossip, conceit, and disorder," and to have to "mourn over many who previously sinned and have not repented of the impurity, sexual immorality, and licentiousness that they have practiced (2 Cor. 12:20–21). Within the Church, opposition arose on the part of heretical teachers, and their audiences had "itching ears" (2 Tim. 4:3). The rich were preferred to the poor (James 2:1–7). Many had withdrawn from the faith (1 Tim. 4:1–3), and norms would have to be established to regulate the conduct of widows and to pass judgment upon charges made against the elders of the Church (1 Tim. 5:3–22).

The Church Vanquishes Sin in Penance

To be sure, the Christian never does battle alone. Salvation is never a private matter between the Christian and God. In virtue of the coming of Jesus Christ into history, a norm of love has been imposed on believers that transcends their private experience. Because believers continue to be bound to that norm, they are still members of the body of Christ. The Church furnishes and interprets the norm of love to which Christians are bound. This norm is not just an external rule. Whatever a Christian does redounds upon all other Christians. "If one member suffers, all members suffer together with it; if one member is honored, all rejoice together with it" (1 Cor. 12:26).

The whole Church is affected by the post-baptismal sin and repentance of its members. As their virtuous actions contribute to the upbuilding of the body of Christ, so sin contributes to its wounding, and, just as in the garden of Paradise sin assaulted the image of God, indeed assaulted God, so today sin assaults the Church.

Penance is an act of the Church. The reparation due for sin includes not only that due in the individual's relationship with God, but also that due the Church, which has been wounded. Just as the Church supports its individual members, suffering for their sins, so the individual sinner, in his or her conversion, must repair the wound inflicted upon the Church. Jesus has given the Church the power of the keys, so that what the Church binds or looses on earth is considered bound or loosed in heaven as well.

The Church is intimately involved with the conversion of baptized but sinful Christians. Besides the wounds within that need to be treated, it possesses an external order that contributes to the edification, the correction, of the faithful.

As mediator of Christ's peace, the Church celebrates the sacrament for the purification and salvation of its sinful members. Through the ministry of the Church, the faithful find Christ's love, and merciful forgiveness. Conversion takes on a concrete form because Christians recognize that salvation reaches them not from within them, but from the historical mediation of Christ, who bestows truth, grace, and love. The Church imposes penances to be performed after sin, not only in order to convey a sense of its gravity and to support penitents in the purification of their lives, but also to indicate that sin has lasting consequences for the wounded body of Christ. Accordingly, penance customarily consists in prayers and good works calculated to "make satisfaction" for the evil committed and to redound to the well-being of the whole Church.

The Sacrament of Penance has assumed various forms in the course of history. In recent centuries attention has focused on private confession. While the communitarian elements are reduced in this form of the sacrament, they remain present in the person of the priest, who represents the Church and Christ. Beginning with Vatican Council II, liturgical elements were then introduced in order to place clearer emphasis on the community aspects of the sacrament. Except in clearly defined emergencies, community liturgical celebrations of Penance do not exempt the penitent from the obligation of individual confession within the broader celebration. In order that the minister of the Church be able to grant forgiveness in the name of Christ, responsibility for all grave sins must be clearly acknowledged and a firm purpose of amendment sincerely expressed. Penitents must submit their sins, and repentance, to the Church, so that the authenticity of their conversion may be acknowledged and confirmed in a public manner. The requisite acknowledgment of responsibility for personal sins is gravely impaired if a personal confession of sins to the confessor is omitted.

The Church's norms require that every Catholic who has committed a serious sin go to confession at least once a year. Of course, the sinner ought to have recourse to confession as soon as possible after the sin. Not only does mortal sin deprive the soul of grace and in case of death would consign the sinner to damnation, but it renders it illicit and invalid for the believer to receive Christ in the Eucharist and impossible to participate fully in the life of the Church.

Sin and Sense of Guilt

The sense of sin, reinforced by confession, must not be confused with a morbid sense of guilt. The authentic sense of sin grows in proportion to our willingness to accept Christ's salvation — to acknowledge that "the blood of Jesus ... cleanses us from all sin" (1 John 1:7). The greater the sense of sin in a Christian, the greater that person's gratitude for forgiveness. Through this forgiveness, Christians live in gladness, since only the divine gift can cleanse from sin. With this increased sense of joy and this gratitude comes a more profound love for God, who has saved the person. And from the roots of a deeper love emerges humility — the recognition that this person could never have had the right to the gift of love.

The modern world is often oppressed by guilt, as we see in literature, art, and, of course, psychology. This is altogether understandable, inasmuch as the sense of guilt issues from a refusal to love.

The year dedicated to reflection on God the Father points up the importance of a catechesis on the sense of sin and God's mercy. John Paul II says it clearly in *Tertio Millennio Adveniente:*

> In this third year, the sense of the "route to the Father" ought to impel all to cling to Christ, the Redeemer of the human race, and to start down a route of authentic *conversion,* which will embrace both a "negative" aspect of deliverance from sin, and a "positive" aspect of choice of the good, expressed by the ethical values contained in the natural law as confirmed and deepened by the Gospel. This is the fitting answer to the rediscovery and renewed celebration of the Sacrament of Penance in its most profound meaning. (*TMA,* 50)

Accordingly, in this year it will be important for us to foster the growth, in our Christian existence, of an openness to an acceptance of grace and forgiveness.

God is a Father, and no sense of guilt is permitted in the divine sight that would close us up in ourselves and in the solitude of anguish. No, in the presence of a Father who loves, we discover how we, too, must be able to love, without allowing selfishness to enter the scene and take control of us.

As we have seen in our commentary on the parable of mercy, God first draws near us; however, we must "enter within ourselves," take account of sin, and make a decision to take once more the path that leads to our Father's house.

Chapter 7

Mary, the Holy Trinity's Sign of Mercy

In Catholic tradition, Mary is immaculate: the creature preserved from all stain of sin by the pure mercy of God. M. D. Philippe declared on the subject:

> Mercy engulfs her from the outset, utterly and completely. All her life long, she ceaselessly receives God's mercy in its fullness. This mercy is intended to introduce her into love, but the love in question takes on a special color, since, when God's love is communicated to a creature, it necessarily takes the form of a merciful love.... Once we grasp that Mary is the ... chef-d'oeuvre of this mercy, we shall to some extent have the key to plumbing and living all of the Father's mercies.

The Father's choice of Mary is founded on the utter gratuity of the divine parental love, which renders her "full of grace" (cf. Luke 1:28, *kecharitōmenē.*) In view of her Messianic motherhood, the Father has poured and infused into her the fullness of the divine mercy. Mary was filled up with grace a priori, as the one chosen to be mother of the incarnate Son of God. Her fullness of grace is the index of her holiness, of her consecration by God, of her mission.

The Fiat and the Magnificat are Mary's response to the Father's mercy. In the Magnificat, Mary sings: "His mercy is for those who fear him from generation to generation.... He has helped his servant Israel, in remembrance of his mercy" (Luke 1:50, 54). Martin Luther, in his commentary on the Magnificat, underscores the humility of the Blessed Virgin vis-à-vis God the Father and places these words on her lips. The

Lord "has seen that I am a little, worthless servant.... It is by his pure mercy that He has willed to look upon a person so despicable, so despised; He could have found a virgin less despicable, a wise, wealthy, powerful one.... God my Savior has looked upon me purely by his grace — on me the contemptible one" (WA 45, 105, 7–106).

Etienne Binet, as well, one of the most noted Mariologists of the seventeenth century, has Mary pronounce words of praise for God's mercy:

> Seeing my humility, or rather my lowliness, and taken with compassion, God has filled me with all of his favors: he has deigned to place everything in someone in whom there had been nothing, and the immensity of his mercies in the immensity of my miseries. The more he fills me up with graces, the more I enter within my nothingness, and ingenuously confess my lack of dignity and my weakness. Hence all generations will proclaim me blessed. It is not by reason of my personal qualities, oh no: of myself I have but me, and that is little enough; but I shall be called blessed because I have received, from the infinite charity of my God, a world of mercies.

The theme of the Magnificat is fundamentally that of the love of the Father for the lowly and the poor. This is why God has chosen for his salvific design a poor and lowly virgin. And with the Magnificat, Mary becomes a sign of the Father's mercy toward all. The Magnificat is the canticle of the valiant woman who vindicates God's rights and who affords a glimpse of the new order to be inaugurated at the coming of the Reign of God.

Mary becomes the prophet of God's mercy, as well as its icon. She as no one else knows the mystery of mercy that reaches its climax on Calvary. The Virgin who became the Mother of Jesus at Christmas, enabling God's mercy to become incarnate, on Calvary becomes the Mother of the Church, expanding her bowels of mercy toward all of her children. For this reason too, the mercy of the Lord will extend from generation to generation, taking on in Mary a twofold connotation: maternal and concrete.

Mary, Mother of Mercy

It is from a point of departure in scriptural data, then, that the Church has so confidently called upon Mary's merciful protection, as an invocation from the close of the third century testifies: "We fly to your mercy." We find numerous testimonials to the clemency, goodness, and mercy of Mary in the first millennium. It would seem to have been James of Saroug (d. 521) who first attributed to Mary the title "Mother of Mercy," a title that then would spread throughout the West, especially in the Middle Ages, as the Marian prayer, the Salve Regina (tenth century), demonstrates. Romanus the Melodist (first half of the sixth century) sings in one of his hymns: "Fittingly, the Merciful one has a merciful Mother."

In the life of Maximus the Confessor (d. 662), published only in 1986, in a reflection on the last years of the Blessed Virgin, we read:

> She bent her mercy not only toward relatives and acquaintances, but toward strangers and enemies, as well, for she was truly the Mother of mercy, the Mother of the Merciful One, . . . the Mother of the One who became incarnate and was crucified for us in order to pour out upon us, his rebellious enemies, his mercy.

In some of the troparia of Andrew of Crete (d. 740), we hear these prayers: "Turn your merciful eye upon my sinful soul: I draw no salvation from works, O Lady Immaculate." "Having washed in the streams of your mercy, O sweet Lady, my soul desiccated with sin, render me fecund in virtue." "Raise up with the wealth of your mercy my soul made miserable by my sins, O Birth-Giver of God." Joseph the Studite (d. 832), brother of the better-known Theodore, in an ode to Mary, prays: "As merciful Mother of God, heal the souls and bodies struck down with passions and sin. For you have conceived and borne Christ, the great physician of bodies and souls, and the inexhaustible font of life."

Fozio (d. ca. 897), prays in an ode:

O bountiful Queen of the World, beseech the One rich in mercy, who became incarnate of your most pure blood, to have pity on me, who have become prey to so many evils. O compassionate one beyond all measure, whose inward parts are sheer mercy, and good beyond all thought, show this to me, Immaculate One, and bestow upon me forgiveness of my numberless transgressions.

(*TPM II*, 865)

Joannes Kyriotis, surnamed the Geometer (d. end of tenth century), in a homily on the Dormition of Mary, offers an exquisite synthesis of our theme:

Surely the Mother of the Merciful One cannot be without mercy. This was evinced, while she was still in life, by her love for the poor, her welcome to all, her intercessions, the healing of soul and body of those who had need of that healing. Now that she has been assumed, her public and private miracles evince the same, in every place, wonders of every kind, above describing, more numerous than the sands of the sea. And again, there are the most exalted and most sublime goods of all, the conversions and continual reconciliations of sinners, the preservation of the path of the just — in a word, the salvation and divinization, common as well as personal, of the race to which she belongs. In such a way,...the One (Christ) who loves human beings so measurelessly becomes still more merciful; the One who, for love, has chosen this woman to nourish human beings, and has established her not only as merciful Mother, but as mediator and reconciler at his side, as well; in such a way, our Advocate with the Father has turned toward us a connatural, irrevocable propensity and affect for another reason, inasmuch as he is constantly besought by another advocate, at his side: the Virgin, who ceaselessly placates his just wrath, and causes his mercies and solicitude to come to all in abundance.

In the West, as well, Mary is commonly called "Mother of Mercy." Such is her title in the eighth century with Paul, Deacon Varnefrido (d. ca. 799), in a homily on the Assumption: "And, as we ascribe it to the Mother of Mercy, she is all mercy for us: she knows how to have compassion for human weaknesses because she knows so well the matter of which we are made. Precisely therefore, she does not cease to intercede for us with her Son" (*TPM III, 755*).

In the life of Odo of Cluny (d. 942/43), we read of a young robber, admitted by Odo to the monastic life, who, three days before his death, had a vision of Mary, who manifested herself as "Mother of Mercy," a title also occurring in Fulbert of Chartres (d. 1028).

In a prayer of the Little Office of Holy Mary (eleventh century), we hear: "Holy Mary, most merciful among all merciful creatures, most holy among the holy, intercede for us. Through you, O Virgin, may our supplications be received by the One who, born of you for us, now reigns in heaven: may his merciful love efface our sins."

According to Saint Bernard (d. 1153), if we fear to have recourse to the mercy of the Father, we can turn to Jesus Christ, become our flesh and our "merciful" Brother. And if even in Jesus we fear the divine majesty, we can have recourse to Mary, our mother and merciful advocate, who gives ear to her children as the Father hears the Son.

Theophanes of Nicea (d. 1381) says of Mary: "She, in truth, and without any fiction, is the divine mercy, for she is filled with bounty, mercy, and sustaining love. . . . She is the vessel that can contain this goodness in all its fullness.... After all, the bowels of the divine mercy are she herself.

In his *Glories of Mary,* Saint Alphonsus (d. 1787) stresses Mary's mercy, and especially her regard and motherly eyes turned toward us. In his commentary on the Salve Regina, the saint places on Mary's lips the following declaration:

> I am called Mother of mercy by all; and indeed God's mercy toward all persons has made me likewise merciful toward them: for that one will be wretched, and wretched everlastingly in the other life, who, with the opportunity of recourse to me who am so compassionate toward all, and who so desire to succor sinners, in wretchedness fails to have that recourse and is damned.

Commenting on the invocation "Turn your eyes of mercy toward us," Saint Alphonsus calls Mary the mother who is "all eyes, to the end that she may hasten to our assistance on this earth." Again, he reports a statement of Richard of Saint Lawrence to the effect that if the eyes of God are turned toward the just (cf. Ps. 33:16), those of Mary are turned toward the just and toward sinners: "For Mary's eyes are a mother's eyes, and a mother regards her little child not only lest he fall, but also that, when he falls, she may hasten to raise him up."

And again: "Saint Bernard wrote that Mary has become all things to all, and opens to all the bosom of her mercy, to the end that all may receive from her, slaves their ransom, the sick their health, the afflicted their comfort, sinners their forgiveness, God his glory; and thereby that no one, Mary being the sun, fail to share her warmth."

Mary "Covenant of Mercy"

In the Ethiopian Church, known for its intense Marian devotion, there is a very old and widespread tradition of a "Covenant of Mercy" (Kidana Meherat) between Jesus and his Mother in behalf of sinners. By calling on the name of

Mary, and celebrating her memory, sinners will be delivered from their every transgression. This pact has actually become a name of Mary in the Ethiopian Church, and is considered the last testament, the "Third Testament" of the divine economy. The feast of Kidana Meherat is celebrated on the sixteenth of Yakatit (corresponding to our February 1), and commemorated on the sixteenth of each month. The account, which we have in various redactions, speaks of Mary being conveyed by the angels, first to Paradise, to contemplate the joy of the redeemed, and then to hell, where sinners were being punished. She was sorely grieved by the lot of those in hell, and prayed incessantly for them. On the sixteenth of the month of Yakatit, when she had gone to Golgatha to pray to her Son, Jesus appeared to her and asked her whether he could grant some desire of hers:

> "What shall I do for you, Mother mine? And what desire of yours do you will that I grant?"
> And Our Lady replied:... "My dear little child and my Savior, my hope and my comfort,... hear my prayer and supplication:... May the one who:

> > Celebrates my memory,
> > builds churches in my name,
> > clothes the naked in my name,
> > visits the sick and gives the hungry to eat and the
> > thirsty to drink,
> > comforts the afflicted and makes glad those who
> > weep,
> > writes my praises,
> > has given his little son or daughter my name,
> > has sung canticles to my name and on every feast of
> > mine:

Grant that one, O Lord, the most beautiful joy, which eye sees not, nor ear hears, nor the human mind imagine!

"I pray and beseech you, O Lord, for all who believe in me: Save them, Lord, from Sheol, remembering the hunger, the thirst, and all of the sufferings that I have endured for you and together with you."

And Our Lord Jesus Christ responded: "Yes, as you have said, I shall fulfill your every desire. Have I not become a human being for this? I swear by my head that this my Covenant will never be violated."

The Ethiopian Church also praises Mary in a literary genre known as *salamta* (plural of *Salam,* "Hail!"), frequently in the form of a litany glorifying the Blessed Virgin's various bodily members, as her head, her neck, her arms. One of these invocations goes: "Salam to your eyes, hung by an able Artisan on the tower of your body! O Mary, font of mercy and clemency! Save me by your word, and deliver me from destruction, for without your succor none can be saved!"

Artistic Celebration

Mary's mercy, besides being praised in the liturgy in its most meaningful form, is also celebrated in art, of East and West alike. Keeping in mind not only the aesthetic and decorative meaning of the Eastern icon, but its profound liturgical and theological content as well, let us recall here the series of icons called, in Russian, the Pokrov ("veil, mantle, protection"), which indicates Mary's motherly protection of the city of her children. The Russian Church has celebrated the Feast of the Pokrov since the beginning of the twelfth century, on October 1, to commemorate Mary's motherly mediation, symbolized by the *maphorion,* the veil of protection spread above the city and over all who turn to her (cf. *RM,* no. 33).

Apropos of an icon of the "protection of Mary," of the school of Novgorod in the fifteenth century, where the representation reached its highest artistic perfection, Trubetskoy wrote:

We see something more than a humanity gathered under the mantle of the Madonna: there is something like a spiritual fusion between the world and the saints gathered here — as if all of that gathering of saints in variegated garments constituted the Madonna's living garment, consecrated by myriad eyes glowing within, gleaming like points of fire.... To her, in pure symmetry, tends from all sides the movement of numberless human eyes.... It is the symmetry of an inspired rainbow about the Queen of Heaven.

Here is one of the prayers from October 1: "Most holy Lady, Virgin Mother of God, cover us with your wondrous mantle, protecting the people from every evil. Truly the admirable Andrew sees you today, as he (saw you when he) prayed in the Church of Blacherne. Today once more, O Our Lady, send us your copious mercy!"

In the icon of the type called the Virgin of Tenderness, Mary is once more represented as Mother of mercy and compassion. This icon emphasizes the profound affection binding the Son to the Mother. The Virgin of Tenderness is a variation of the Brephokratousa, the Madonna who "lifts her Infant" to her cheek, and places sentiments of motherly tenderness on Mary's face. Her head, slightly bent toward the Child, indicates an attitude of protection. The first appearance of this image at Constantinople goes back to the eleventh or twelfth century, the earliest moments of the existence of at least two churches dedicated to the Panagia Eleousa, our Merciful All-Holy Lady. Actually, the inscription "Eleousa" rarely occurs on the icon. The name is given in many variations, the most familiar of which is the Glycophilousa, "Sweet and Loving," whence the name, "Virgin of Tenderness." In this icon, Mary embraces and clasps to herself with motherly tenderness the Baby Jesus. The emphasis is on the affection binding Mother to Child and their great trust: the baby places his cheek upon that of the mother and seems to be giving her a kiss.

Another icon of this type is the celebrated "Vladimirskaya" (Madonna of Vladimir), cited by the Pope in *Redemptoris Missio*, no. 33. This icon, celebrated liturgically for different reasons at least three times a year (May 21, June 23, August 26), is an artistically very successful version of the Glycophilousa, with certain traits of the Odigitria. Mary lifts her Child with her right arm as the Child embraces her, cheek to cheek, and regards her with tenderness. But the Virgin has her head at an angle, in a protective attitude, while her eyes are directed ahead and her left hand indicates to the faithful her divine Son. Restored after the October Revolution and freed of the *riza* — the gilded garment studded with precious stones, a true chef-d'oeuvre of goldwork — the icon has revealed all of its artistic and spiritual splendor. It is one of the pinnacles of Byzantine Marian iconography: "It may be the most beautiful Marian icon, and dearest to the Russians, whose whole history it has accompanied." In the Office of the feast of August 26, Russians fly to Mary's merciful protection:

Today, shining and beautiful, the glorious city of Moscow receives your miraculous, dawn-like icon, O sovereign Lady! To it we fly, and we your suppliants invoke you thus: "O wondrous Queen, Mother of God, pray Christ, our God incarnate of you, to preserve this city, and all Christian cities and climes, free of danger, and to save our souls, for he is merciful!"

Western art, as well, knows the canvasses of Our Lady of Mercy. They, too, are characterized by Mary's open mantle protecting her faithful. Gregory of Tours popularized in the West the legend of the Jewish baby saved from the flames by Mary's mantle. Substantially the same content is expressed in the images of the Pietà and the Immaculate Heart of Mary. There are even those who have found, in Michelangelo's *Last Judgment* itself, a most significant allusion to Mary's mercy, which softens the atmosphere of severity that seems to reign in the Sistine Chapel.

Our consideration of Mary brings us to what John Paul II has written on his own account apropos of the year devoted to the theme of God the Father:

> In all of this ample assignment of tasks, Mary Most Holy, the Father's daughter of predilection, will be present to the regard of the faithful as the perfect example of love of God and neighbor alike. . . . The Father has chosen Mary for a unique mission in salvation history — that of being the mother of "the long-awaited Savior. The Virgin has responded to God's call with full availability: "Here am I, the servant of the Lord" (Luke 1:38). Her motherhood, begun at Nazareth and lived to the fullest on the hill outside Jerusalem at the foot of the cross, will be felt in this year as an affectionate, pressing invitation addressed to God's children to return to their Father's house, as they hear her motherly voice: "Do what Christ tells you" (cf. John 2:5). (TMA, 54)

Chapter 8

Charity

Following the guidelines of John Paul II, we here insert a chapter devoted to the subject of charity. The Pontiff writes in *Tertio Millennio Adveniente:*

> It will be in order, especially in this year, to set in relief the theological virtue of *charity*, recalling the pregnant synthesis of the First Letter of John: "God is love" (1 John 4:8, 16). Charity, in its twin visage of love for God and love for neighbor, is the synthesis of the believer's moral life. That life has its wellspring and destination in God.
>
> *(TMA, 50)*

It will be well, then, for us to reflect, in these pages, on the subject of charity.

Love is the beginning and the end of the way that leads to God. As Scripture proclaims, God is love: it is the Father who eternally generates his Son in the bond of personal love that is the Holy Spirit. The world has been created in order that free creatures be introduced into the communion of the Trinitarian love. Not even sin destroyed God's plan; if anything, it intensified it. God has shown how far the divine initiatives in behalf of creatures will go: to the very cross. Although it belongs to the nature of love to empty itself for the beloved, sin has led God to manifest the full extent of this self-emptying. Love is not only the ecstasy of joy that unites the lover to the beloved. Love is also the painful sacrifice in which is experienced the depth of self-abandonment and rejection. Jesus on the cross experienced not only the hatred of his enemies, but also the abandonment and betrayal of his very friends. All the more terrible was his sense of desolation before the Father: "My God, my God, why have you forsaken me?" (Mark 15:34; Ps. 22:1). The divine plan of salvation, incarnated by Jesus, which aimed at uniting God and the human being, seemed to be headed for ruin. All that Jesus had proclaimed, everything he had lived for, was a failure. God was being rejected, precisely by the persons for whom he was offering his life.

Jesus never despaired. He knew from within the infinite love of his Father. Indeed, that love constituted his very being and personal identity. He was and always will be the Son of the Father, the child of that Father's love (Col. 1:13), and he cannot fail to bear witness of the Father's love. Even the verse from the Psalms that Jesus quotes to express his anguish was a statement inspired by God and placed on the psalmist's lips in anticipation of the cross. Jesus knew that that cry constituted only the beginning of the psalm. On his lips, it is transformed into a prayer of supreme trust in God and certitude of deliverance. Thus, faced with death and the seeming victory of sin, Jesus cast his reliance on infinite love and his Father's concern: "Father, into your hands I commend my spirit" (Luke 23:46). And he actually uttered the cry of victory: "It is finished" (John 19:30).

By Jesus' death on the cross, God's plan was attained and accomplished. God's holiness and majesty seemed infinitely distant in the tortured figure broken on the cross — the "curse" dying under God's law that the law of sin might not prevail (cf. Gal. 3:13). What alone could unite absolute rejection with God's transcendent glory was love: God. Indeed, the very force of the contrast between what human beings expected of the holiness of God and the abandonment of the cross makes God's love even more resplendent. Nothing is exempt from the power of God's love, no sinner can be regarded as abandoned by God now that the Son has become "sin" for love of God (2 Cor. 5:21).

God's self-emptying on the cross was God's victory. The Son emptied himself in his humanity to be filled up by the Father — the reflection in the reign of sin of what occurs throughout eternity. The resurrection is the manifestation of the total penetration of Jesus' human nature by God's love. His body was glorified and since that moment exists in the Church. The Church is God's great gift to humanity. It represents the concretization of love, God's condescension to the conditions of our freedom so that we are able to accept the divine love. More than this: the Church reveals God's initiative in our behalf. The Church, which exists before ourselves, proclaims and renders present the crucified and risen love of God that we may be able to respond to it by accepting it and allowing it to steep our lives.

Primacy of Love

Love is the central mystery of Christianity. But it is not a mere objective mystery, set forth before passive observers. The divine love intends to be communicated to the heart of the human being, and to animate it. The divine love is the power that gives the Church its life and structure. The Church of Corinth was internally shaken by competition for prestige and a sense of rank to which Christians laid claim on the basis of the charisms that they had received. Saint Paul reminds these persons of the essentials of the Christian life in the famous chapter that constitutes a hymn to love:

> If I speak in the tongues of mortals and of angels, but do not have love, I am a noisy gong or a clanging cymbal. And if I have prophetic powers, and understand all mysteries and all knowledge, and if I have all faith, so as to remove mountains, but do not have love, I am nothing. If I give away all my possessions, and if I hand over my body so that I may boast, but do not have love, I gain nothing.
>
> Love is patient; love is kind; love is not envious or boastful or arrogant or rude. It does not insist on its own way; it is not irritable or resentful; it does not rejoice in

wrongdoing, but rejoices in the truth. It bears all things, believes all things, hopes all things, endures all things.

Love never ends. But as for prophecies, they will come to an end; as for tongues, they will cease; as for knowledge, it will come to an end. For we know only in part, and we prophesy only in part; but when the complete comes, the partial will come to an end. When I was a child, I spoke like a child, I thought like a child, I reasoned like a child; when I became an adult, I put an end to childish ways. For now we see in a mirror, dimly, but then we will see face to face. Now I know only in part; then I will know fully, even as I have been fully known. And now faith, hope, and love abide, these three; and the greatest of these is love. (1 Cor. 13:1–13)

It is easy to recognize in this chapter from Saint Paul the spirit of the Beatitudes preached by Our Lord. The Beatitudes are at the beginning of Jesus' message in the Gospel of Saint Matthew and describe the spirit that ought to prevail in the Reign of God. How different from worldly wisdom is the spirit of Jesus Christ! Jesus praises, and regards as blessed, the poor of spirit, the afflicted, the meek, those who hunger and thirst for justice, the merciful, the poor of heart, the peacemakers, those who are persecuted for justice' sake (Matt. 5:3–10). The basis of his preaching was not ordinary human wisdom, which is ambiguous at best, and at worst would counsel us to draw the most immediate advantages from this world. Jesus, by contrast, opposes the wisdom of the world, because his source of experience transcended this world. He knew himself and the Father and from this experiential knowledge could judge the world aright. He relativized the demands of the world because he knew the creative power of God's love. The love of God, poured forth into the hearts of the human being, must resist selfishness and reestablish the values willed by God. The Church of Jesus' disciples is obviously the locus par excellence in which the spirit of the Reign ought to prevail. Inevitably, conflict will arise between the Church and the world. The Spirit of Jesus animates the Church, but the world has other criteria.

The Theological Virtues

The Christian life has no other meaning and aim than love. It is structured by the three theological virtues of faith, hope, and love. When all other things have passed, as Saint Paul writes, these remain established, and the greatest is love. When all is said and done, faith and hope are contained in love. The Christian faith declares, in the face of sin and death, that love is stronger than death and sin. Its confidence is based on a knowledge of the fact of Jesus' resurrection. All of the dogmas of the Church have the purpose of supporting the truth of this fact by recognizing the structure and implications of incarnate Love crucified and risen. Love is not a vague feeling or a generic philanthropic benevolence. In order to love, there must be a definite structure that the human mind can grasp. The Christian message shows a profound unity rooted in the love of God: the Love that has become a human being and the Love that is still present in the Church under the appearances of bread and wine.

Christian hope, for its part, trusts in the final victory of love in individuals and in history. What makes hope and faith so difficult is the so differentiated panorama presented by the world: the world has not yet been transformed into a transparent sign of the love of God. Nonetheless, if the Love professed by faith is authentic, it ought to transform the world and the persons who inhabit it. Love manifests God's omnipotence, since it calls human beings to abandon all for love. Only the humility of God in the face of the freedom of the human being and the patience of God before that being's sin have delayed the universalization of the victory of Easter morning. It is the will of God that human freedom be transformed into the image of the divine Son, and cooperate with the divine plan of salvation. At the end of time, however, the victory of Love will be guaranteed and manifested in full power. The omnipotence of Love will have prevailed.

Faith is empty, and hope vain, unless the believer experiences love in the Church of Christ. Between the past event, which is the basis of hope, and the future accomplishment of hope, the Church must strive to serve as a bridge. Only if charity is experienced in the present, in the Church, does faith have eyes to see and rightly interpret the past event and the courage to keep up the struggle of hope against the appearances of this world.

Mystery of Love

Love is the greatest of all mysteries. Everyone wishes to be loved and to know that there is a meaning in his or her life. All think they know what love is, since in some way they have been loved by their parents or someone else. Even in the worst scenario: love must have been proclaimed by its absence, as it is a boon desired by every heart. But notwithstanding the seeming universality of the knowledge of love, love remains a mystery, because it is withdrawn from the control of the beloved. Reason can neither impose love, nor explain it once it is bestowed. No one who is the object of love can discover any justification of the fact of receiving a total devotion, a commitment in which the lover guarantees to be faithful to the point of preferring the beloved to himself or herself to the very death.

All persons seek love; and yet the gift of love is always more than what they have expected or hoped for. In its full sense, it implies a sharing in the very life of God, an infinitude of Self-bestowal on the beloved. No desire or hope on the part of the human being can remain unfulfilled when God consigns the divine self to human beings in love. Human beings must only open themselves to love and permit it to penetrate ever more deeply into their hearts. Finally the justified will be taken up without reserve into the mystery of Love without

limit and receive the power to respond without reserve, empty-
ing themselves fully in order to find themselves once more fully
in God.

Temptations against Love

As the mystery of charity will at last explain all things in heaven
and on earth, so even now it sheds more than enough light to
guide us through the dark meanderings of this life. Love surely
captivates all persons, and its eternal promises would be irre-
sistible, were it not for all of the sufferings of life. Not only
does death threaten all that we are, have, and regard as dear,
but even an empirical, sociological study of human behavior
scarcely demonstrates that self-sacrificing love is the prime mo-
tive of human activity. This is all the more true in view of the
fact that sociologists tend to reduce human motivation to the
lowest common denominator, and seek the reasons for behavior
in the fundamental human penchant for pleasure, possessions,
and power. With so much suffering in the world, when even the
best-laid plans and intentions are frustrated, how can human
beings be sure that love is the meaning of existence and that a
loving God takes care of them? Faced with the absence of love
that characterizes their experience, a world in which persons
are wolves to one another, a world in which human beings
reciprocally manipulate one another, some either reject the existence of God or declare that God is irrelevant for the solution
of the human being's problems on earth.

Christian Meaning of Suffering

For a Christian, the pain and anguish of existence do not de-
rive simply from finitude. Creation is good, and God creates
finite beings. The finite limit surely furnishes the possibility of
suffering. Having a body means being able to stumble. Being a
limited spirit includes freedom and the possibility of rejection
on the part of others, as well as, conversely, an evil personal

use of freedom with the consequences flowing therefrom. To preclude all possibilities of suffering would mean to abolish finitude and make the human being God — that is, to yield to the original temptation of Eden and attempt the impossible. The possibility of suffering, however, is not an evil in itself. A world without the possibility of suffering would be utterly tedious, a world without challenge or achievement. Knights would grow rusty and peevish, having no dragons from which to save damsels in distress. At the same time, it is necessary that the dragons include authentic dangers. Love desires self-gift and the accomplishment of something as a gift for the beloved. Since the degree of "suffering" in any undertaking is determined partly by the way in which it is perceived, the "sufferings" of Eden would be relatively minor. The blows in a game of football or rugby are scarcely felt in the enthusiasm of the struggle for one's team. In fact, the next day, the bruises can be pointed to as a sign of pride!

The horror of gratuitous, meaningless suffering has entered the world only with sin, which has destroyed the natural unity among human beings and made the world, in the best of hypotheses, an ambiguous sign of God's love. Now the human being is found to be at odds with the others, *homo homini lupus,* and the reasons for self-sacrifice are no longer clear. Everything and everyone have become a threat to the individual, to his or her well-being and even existence. The Christian, however, knows that each must suffer for the others. It is impossible to separate oneself from one's brothers and sisters in Adam, and any attempt in this direction only has the consequence of an increase in evil in the world, in lack of love. For the Christian, suffering is a mystery even more than for the noble Buddhist bodhisattvas, who postpone personal illumination and beatitude to show themselves compassionate, to share the sufferings of others, and to allow their desires to be fulfilled in them. The Christian knows that desires can be good, inasmuch as they arise from creation; but concupiscence can impose upon them an erroneous orientation. Indeed, the Christian sees in suffering a positive invitation to join Christ and to contribute to the salvation of the world. Love unites a person with the beloved, in the desire to share the other's lot. Is there a mother who, faced with the suffering of her child, would rather be a mere onlooker than suffer with her child? How much more, then, ought this to be the attitude of a person before God, who has suffered for our sins! If Jesus has suffered for the Christian, ought not the Christian desire to share Jesus' sufferings? Scripture assures us that the Christian can and does share his sufferings.

To preach the Gospel in a hostile world almost necessarily includes suffering. Jesus has foretold it: "If they persecuted me, they will persecute you (John 15:20; cf. Matt. 10:25). "Servants are not greater than their master (John 13:16; cf. Matt. 10:24). The price of glory with Christ is suffering with Christ (Rom. 8:17; 2 Tim. 2:11–12; Acts 14:22). Communion (*koinōnia*), established and manifested with the greatest clarity in the Eucharist, includes a participation in the sufferings of Christ (Phil. 3:10; 1 Pet. 4:13). In fact, "the sufferings of Christ are abundant for us" (2 Cor. 1:5), writes Saint Paul. The Apostle undergoes many sufferings — the "death of Jesus" (2 Cor. 4:10), for love of Christians, who in their turn share in his sufferings (2 Cor. 1:6–7; 4:8–12; Eph. 3:13). And again Paul writes: "I am now rejoicing in my sufferings for your sake, and in my flesh I am completing what is lacking in Christ's afflictions for the sake of his body, that is, the church" (Col. 1:24). The Apostle is saying not that there is something lacking in the passion of Christ, but that something is lacking by way of participation in that passion. There is no definitive opposition between Jesus' sufferings and ours. Precisely as the indicative of God's activity does not destroy, but founds, the imperative addressed to us, as the divine omnipotence does not annul human freedom but reinforces it, as God's infinity does not preclude the existence of finite essences, but creates them, so the sufferings of Christ posit the foundation of the meaning of human suffering. Joined to Christ in love, the believer suffers for others, for all sinners to whom the believer is joined through Adam, as for all those justified in the body of Christ. After all, everything that any member of the body of Christ does or suffers redounds upon all of the other members (1 Cor. 12:26). Through suffering, love is purified and grows. Thus, individual members who spontaneously accept their suffering in union with Christ not only grow in grace, but they also contribute to the increase and effectiveness of love in the Church, which is the instrument of salvation for all. In this fashion, even that which, at first blush, seems most opposed to God's will, suffering, is taken up into the divine plan and rendered capable of praising God.

For Christians, there is nothing in their experience that can separate them from God (Rom. 8:35–39). Everything, suffering or gladness, can serve an increase in love and build up the body of Christ (Eph. 2:22–23; 4:16; Col. 2:19). Thus, through the cross, the dross of suffering is transmuted into the gold of grace and glory, and the natural order, through grace, attains in greater measure the destiny of union with God that was originally intended for it. Like nature and freedom, so also nature and grace need not be ranged against each other. Grace presumes nature, while nature is corrected, preserved, and lifted above itself by grace.

Love of God and Love of Neighbor

If love is the beginning and end of all of the ways of the Lord, love ought to be the beginning and end of the human being's paths as well. In becoming a human being, God joined the lot of the human being to his own, granting to that being a share in the endless divine life. From that moment forward, on earth as in heaven, no one can love God without loving the human being who is the divine image, nor love the human being without loving God. The First Letter of John establishes this truth in unequivocal fashion:

Beloved, let us love one another, because love is from God; everyone who loves is born of God and knows God. Whoever does not love does not know God, for God is love. God's love was revealed among us in this way: God sent his only Son into the world so that we might live through him. In this is love, not that we loved God, but that he loved us and sent his Son to be the atoning sacrifice for our sins. Beloved, since God loved us so much, we also ought to love one another. No one has ever seen God; if we love one another, God lives in us, and his love is perfected in us. (1 John 4:7–12)

Saint John wrote this exhortation to Christians who shared the life of Christ. In the family that is the Church, Jesus' sisters and brothers ought to love one another, because the God of love dwells in them. Indeed, God dwells in them to the extent that they love one another reciprocally, so closely are love of God and love of one's siblings intertwined. An analogous relationship can be seen among non-Christians. Saint Paul included them in the circle of Christian love: "Whenever we have an opportunity, let us work for the good of all, and especially for those of the family of faith" (Gal. 610). Inasmuch as God wills that all persons be saved and come to a knowledge of the truth (1 Tim. 2:4), the divine love extends to them, and Christians have the duty of spreading the truth about Jesus, in word and in the testimonial of life (Matt. 28:19–20; Luke 24:47–48; Acts 1:8).

The love that comes first from Christ, and the Christian's love that responds to it, are not vague feelings. They include a definite task and manifest a basic structure that can be recognized and realized in the Church, the body of Christ. Only from this center do persons find the strength for total dedication to God and to the needs of their siblings. This truth is demonstrated in the most incontestable manner in the case of the Virgin Mary, who consecrated her very life to her Son, so that the Church sees in her the perfect form of the realization of this truth.

Chapter 9

The Our Father

The Our Father is the prayer that Jesus has willed to leave his disciples. It signs the point of arrival of a long journey, which gradually led, under Jesus' wise guidance, to a grasp of the coherent relationship that the baptized ought to have with God. For all Christians, it is a sacred prayer, not only because it has issued from the very lips of Jesus, but because he has willed that in it the originality of faith in him should become manifest. Jesus is the necessary path of access to God, and through him, who is the Son, we too are enabled to turn to God and call God Father.

Rightly does the *Catechism of the Catholic Church* conclude with an explanation of the Our Father. The reason is clear: the core content of the faith and all of the teaching of the Church are condensed in the prayer that Jesus taught his disciples. And when we, as well, recite this prayer daily, it is as if we were professing a synthesis of the entire gospel; in it, indeed, we acknowledge Jesus' revelation and declare our belief in his unsurpassable love.

The most familiar liturgical text of the Our Father — the one we normally use — adopts the formulation proposed by the Gospel of Matthew (Matt. 6:9–13), which we find inserted in the great Sermon on the Mount (Matt. 5–7).[4] In order to grasp it, we must first of all attend to the context, then to the text that expresses it, and finally to the implications that it contains and are developed elsewhere in Matthew's ambience.

The context of the Our Father is the Sermon on the Mount.

---

4. In the following pages we have made extensive use of the commentary on the Our Father by Ugo Vanni. In fact, we have thought it appropriate that our text make explicit reference to that work, as our own is intended as a catechetical aid in preparation for the Great Jubilee of the year 2000. We take this occasion to express our thanks to the author.

This in itself is a meaningful fact. The Sermon on the Mount is a relatively complete program of Christian practice, based on the Beatitudes, with which it opens (Matt. 5:3–11). The Beatitudes represent Jesus' value judgments on the human being's fundamental choices, on the valid or invalid aspects of persons' lives. A good three chapters develop these basic points, detail them, and apply them to various situations. Among the concrete situations forming the object of a more concrete application, we find that of typically Christian prayer. Such prayer will not have that extroverted, horizontal attitude that occasionally constituted a degeneration of the Jewish prayer — and others — of the time. Jesus insists that prayer be addressed "to your Father who sees in secret" (Matt. 6:6). Christian prayer comes forward as a dialogue stamped with an intense filial intimacy, unfolding between the Christian and God. Precisely because it is a dialogue between two persons, it is understood practically in passing: it is not necessary to multiply words, "as" — it is explicitly noted — "the Gentiles do" (Matt. 6:7). There was probably a tendency to verbosity in Matthew's church community, which must have been reflected in prayer as well. Instead the Christian rapport with the Father is spare, essential, and strikes to the heart of the matter. This is the specific context in which the Our Father is situated. The context qualifies it as an exquisitely Christian prayer, which, as it were, leaves the human heart and flies to the heart of God. It is this essentiality, this depth, this openness not always susceptible of conceptualization, that characterizes a mature relationship with the Father.

Let us now look more closely at how this prayer, the one characteristic of the Christian, is articulated. We find the original presentation of the formula of the Our Father in Matthew (6:9–13) and in Luke (11:2–4).

Our Father, Who Art in Heaven

Let us commence our analysis with Matthew. The Christian prayer is addressed to God, calling God "Father." In Jesus' am-

bience, and that of the first disciples, the term resonates above
all with a social character. It is the father who, with a sense
of responsibility and solicitude, organizes family life and pro-
vides individuals with that of which they have need (cf. Matt.
13:52). The entire family gravitates about the father, about
his industriousness, his abilities, his courage, his wisdom. One
turns to God because one feels at home, along with all of the
other persons of the home, in the consciousness that God as
Father is concerned for us, and adequately so.

Along with the phenomenology that sees the father located
in the collective ambience of the family, the strictly inter-
subjective relationship deserves to be emphasized. The father
is also the one who comprehends, the one who does his rear-
ing as a person, the one who understands the child, the one in
whom the child has an utter confidence. The figure of the father, understood in this twofold dimension, is applied to God.
Christians, calling God Father, forthrightly feel joined to God
in a family situation — and, furthermore, feel loved and understood to the bottom of their heart. God is indeed "your Father
who sees in secret" (Matt. 6:6).

The collective aspect is the one that is emphasized: "Our
Father" are the opening words, with a reference to the socio-
familial dimension that Christians are acquiring. It may be an
admonition to the Matthean community in view of certain cen-
trifugal tendencies. At all events, the emphasis is on the fact
that Christians find themselves living together, not just as a
social aggregate, but in virtue of a thread uniting them, with
which they are shot through in their most intimate and personal values. The Father "who sees in secret" is also the Father
who sees all Christians in a unitary glance.

God, thought of and felt in the categories of Father in
earthly experience, nevertheless remains on the divine transcendent level. But the divine transcendency does not diminish the
divine parenthood. On the contrary: we can even say that God
multiplies the divinity by the parenthood and the parenthood
by the divinity. Thus there is a God who is infinitely Father

and a Father who is Father to the infinite degree. All of this is indicated by the expression "who art in heaven." "Heaven" signifies the plane proper to God, underscoring God's unattainable reality. It is also an admonition to avoid any banalization: there could have been the risk, in approaching God as Father, not to feel God too near — this never occurs — but to consider God, so to speak, in a reduced form, projecting upon God the categories of experience, inevitably limited, of earthly parenthood. Matthew warns us of this risk and puts us on our guard against it by counterbalancing the level of the human being with the level of the one whom, to use a typically Matthean expression, he calls "the heavenly Father."

Hallowed Be Thy Name

The first petition addressed to the heavenly Father regards the divine name: may your name be hallowed, sanctified. A certain specification can clarify very simply the line of this petition. In the biblical cultural ambience, the name stands for the person and is never reducible to a pure denomination. The imposition or change in a name indicates a change in the subject, a qualification in view of a mission to accomplish, a new capacity conferred. The name manifests and expresses what the person is and is comprehensible only in terms of the ambience of the person himself or herself. In petitioning the Father that the divine name be hallowed, we ask God that God's very person be sanctified.

At this point the problem arises of the meaning of "hallowing." The semantic field to which the term belongs refers strictly to the divinity: it indicates what is proper to, typical of, God. One wonders, then, how a sanctification with regard to God can be conceived. The risk of a vicious circle, a discourse simply void of meaning, has suggested the alternative of interpreting "hallowing," sanctifying, not in the sense of an ontological characterization referrable to God, but in the sense of an acknowledgment. In this case, we would be able to say that "thy name," thyself, is acknowledged as holy. This is a widespread interpretation. But the verb "to hallow," to sanctify, never denotes, in biblical usage, a merely cognitive reference that would blur into an acknowledgment. What is referred to is an action: in the active voice, "to hallow" means to render holy, to render like unto God; in the passive voice, it stresses the effect of this homogenization produced and realized in respect of God. The same problem arises, then, and there might seem to be no way out of it: How is it possible to hallow the Hallowed One, to divinize God? We are furnished a solid basis for a response in Ezekiel: "I will sanctify my great name, which has been profaned among the nations, and which you have profaned among them; and the nations shall know that I am the Lord, says the Lord God, when through you I display my holiness before their eyes" (Ezek. 36:23).

This passage from Ezekiel, especially given the close contact between Matthew and the entire Old Testament, is enlightening. The sanctification spoken of is real and refers, in parallelism, first to the name of God, who is speaking, then actually to God, but by way of an ever more widespread participation of this sanctity, this holiness, as imparted to the people. According to this interpretation, God our Father is asked to see to the realization of the divine holiness and its spread throughout the great Christian family.

Thy Kingdom Come

The subsequent petition regards God's Reign, the Reign of the Father who is in heaven. In order to grasp the meaning of this expression, we shall have to hark back to the theology of the Bible, to examine the Reign that we find prevailing in the Old Testament itself and then converging in the New. The "Reign of God" is not limited to the dominion belonging to God in respect of all creation, but implies a series of initiatives regarding God and the human being which can be synthesized as follows. First of all there is a descending movement: God in some sense emerges from the divine inaccessibility and, encountering the human being, offers that human being an initiative. Here is the understanding between God and the human being, the "covenant," as it was explicitly called, that involves a bilateral proposition: God makes a commitment in behalf of the human being, but asks the human being to observe the commandments in exchange. At this point, an ascending movement enters the scene: human beings emerge from their profane, secular level and dare to encounter God in an attitude of available reciprocity. Taking note of the offer that comes to them from God, human beings say their own yes. The meeting of the two lines, descending and ascending, determines a new situation, which will comport a connected, closer sharing between God and the human being, all but a symbiosis: this new reality is called a reign and is already actual in the Old Testament, at least beginning with the covenant of Sinai. As far as the New Testament is concerned, along the descending line God, who is revealed as Father, offers the human being the wealth of Christ, and in the ascending line the human being, taking note of this new, augmented gift, opens to it completely by way of the yes of faith. The new situation, thus determined, is the Reign of God in its typical New Testament acceptation.

As we see, there is a development, a passage from the Old Testament to the New. But once the level of the New Testament is reached, there is a further impulse: the "reign" will involve a presence of Christ, ever more compenetrating, in all reality, in persons and in things, and, by way of Christ, an ever closer and more reconciled presence on the part of God. The ultimate term of this movement under way will be the eschatological goal, in which, as Paul recalls, God will be "all in all" (1 Cor. 15:28). The Reign viewed in this conclusive phase belongs to the future, in the essential sense of being strictly eschatological.

Now let us return to our text. When the Christian asks that the Reign of the Father "come," the appeal is by way of anticipation of this development. What is sought is a greater presence of the riches of Christ among human beings — in their life, in their structures, in the world in which they live. The petition regards both God and the human being, precisely because God has willed to become involved with the human being by way of the divine gift of the presence of Christ.

Thy Will Be Done

Another petition presented to the Father regards the realization of the divine will. The Father's will is understood in the objective sense: it is a matter of all that God has intended for the human being. This means especially the commandments, all of the indications deriving for the human being from the word spoken by God, incarnate in Christ, and interpreted by the Spirit. Further, given that God the Creator organizes the movement of history as well and does everything in function of the human being, we can say that a message expressing an element of the divine will is also found enclosed in the history of individuals. To do the will of God entails a full executive docility with respect to the broad spectrum thus manifested.

The petition addressed to the Father that the divine will be done is not an act of passive resignation. It involves a sharing of hearts. Christians realize that their good lies precisely in what God proposes them. This produces the desire — after all, there is no true prayer without desire — to do the divine will. This realization involves, on the one side, God, as the one who loves human beings, protects them, and ardently desires their full realization; and on the other side, it involves human beings, who recognize in trepidation and joy that God their Father follows them moment by moment, cares for them, and manifests to them the divine will on the strength of that love. The upshot, for the Christian, is the ideal of an adequate execution, a realization that, from a point of departure on the human level, will reach the very plane of God, and will bring upon earth, the human being's own level, the totality proper to heaven, which is the plane of God. In this sense, the actualization of the will of God will be realized on earth, but elevating it to an optimal level of transcendent perfection, something of God, a relationship with heaven.

Give Us This Day Our Daily Bread

The petition for bread, "Give us this day our daily bread," stands at the center of the seven petitions of the Matthean Our Father. It too is the one that appears as very characteristic of the Christian who addresses God as Father. It is proper to a father to give his children bread. Indeed, the petition for bread returns us to the framework of the family life in which the figure of the father is located. Bread, in the biblical cultural orbit, is at once concrete reality and symbol. In realistic language, bread is the basic aliment of life. God our Father, in the divine concern for the development of human beings' life in the concretion of their history, takes to heart the alimentation that renders this possible. That consideration is reinterpreted here in the focus of the family. The food asked of God is no longer merely the fruit of trees (Gen. 1:29), but is bread, the foodstuff made by the human being for the human being and divided among the family members. Addressing themselves to God specifically as Father, then, and relying precisely on God's family parenthood, Christians ask God for the food that enables them to live.

But bread is also a symbol. As such, it evokes an image of the other things that serve their life in space and time, everything that makes family life not only possible, but also pleasant. This will be clothes, a roof over one's head, in sum, everything in one's environment that, while it is secondary to food, contributes to the living of life with serenity and dignity.

Bread is asked today and for today. There is a double emphasis on the daily, then, and this is significant. It supposes that, as Father, God follows, with a care worthy of God and worthy of the children of the divine care, the development of their life, a life in space and time. The Father's care, then, will follow the children always and everywhere, without the slightest breach in continuity. It is precisely this living, ever simultaneous, relationship with the Father that moves the children to ask, moment by moment, occasion by occasion, place by place, what is needful and useful for their existence. They do not seek to amass treasures on earth, or even to store up provisions against the unforeseeable circumstances of the future, closing themselves up in human calculations. Christians are able to live day by day, because they know that day by day they are followed, loved, guided, protected by the Father, and never too early or too late.

Finally, the familiar framework in which the petition is posited connotes the completeness of the family. The bread asked for is "ours," not "mine." It is everyone's bread, and reaches all. We ask it for one another. The family spirit suggested by the biblical figure of fatherhood involves, as we have repeatedly stressed, a horizontal reciprocity among Christian siblings as well. They should at the same time feel themselves to be children of the Father. This realization will now transport them in their reciprocity to an attitude of respect for the vertical attitude that the Father has toward them.

Forgive Us Our Trespasses

Christians are conscious that they have committed, vis-à-vis God, "trespasses" to be atoned for, or, as Matthew would have it, "debts" to be paid. The symbolic image expresses a sorrowful reality: the void, the lacuna, the insufficiency that even Christians can posit, in the ambience of their existence, through their wrong choices, their "sins."

Human beings owe what God bestows upon them. Thus, an omission regarding the context of the reality and value devised by God becomes a debt — according to the symbolic image used — that human beings first of all owe themselves. But God is Father, and Father to the infinite degree, and so takes personally any, shall we say, embezzlement of love in the form of evil committed by human beings, albeit always to their own loss.

This process of "embezzlement" of love takes on more precise delineaments when, for example, there is question of covenant, commandments, law, always coming from God and always being the expression of the divine will of love. God as Father takes the human being seriously, and wishes to be taken seriously by human beings. If, then, what God asks of the human being — always to their advantage — goes unrealized, a void is formed that actually touches God. A breach is effected in the intersubjectivity of the two. God as Father comes forth to meet human beings: God overcomes the breaches and fills up these human voids. In terms of the metaphor we are using, God remits debts. And God wishes human beings to ask for this remission so that they may become aware of what is at stake.

We have seen how our relationship with God as Father is realized in the concretion of a family. Christians have other children of God by their side, their siblings. And since God's attitude with regard to individuals is the example to follow, Christians must produce in the horizontal rapport with them that which they receive in the vertical. Consequently, the "voids" around them, in their reciprocal relationships — the breaches, everything that dissolves in the presence of a commitment not maintained, that constitutes a lacuna, a lack of goodness, of attention, of assistance, of love with regard to one another — constitute a list of horizontal "debts" that must be eliminated as if one wishes to eliminate the "debt" with regard to God. Otherwise, the flow of goodness that begins with God and seeks to steep human beings, thence to return to God, will simply be blocked.

With respect to the horizontal level, human beings move in the human field. Helpless to fill up the voids that divide them from God, to "pay their debts" to God, Christian persons can do so with regard to the other human beings found on their own plane. And they must do so. It is a "family" demand on the part of God as Father, who seeks to be imitated in this constructive goodness carried to all extremes. Consequently, in order to be able to invoke God as Father, Christian persons will first have to extend their hand to their siblings. God, it could be said, is unwilling to be invoked outside this collective family orbit, and rebuffs anyone who would attempt to reach him alone, excluding others. Conversely, by doing unto others as they would have others do unto them, and, with regard to the "debts" contracted, remitting, remedying, reconstructing all of the malformations effected in the horizontal rapport, the Christian will be sure of being heard by the Father.

Lead Us Not into Temptation, but Deliver Us from (the) Evil (One)

The last two petitions of the Our Father still bear on the mystery of sin, as seen in those elements that constitute its so ready occasion: temptation and the evil one.

The biblical concept of temptation is a special one, and, more than a concept in the strict sense, is an agglomerate of concepts. A temptation occurs when certain values originally embraced, individually or collectively, come under pressure. This may be an individual or a collective pressure, a momentary or a protracted one. The clearest exemplification is in the sojourn in the desert dividing the flight from Egypt from the entry into the land of promise. There are forty years of temptations in the wilderness. The values of the covenant, proposed to the people and accepted by them, come under manifold pressure: the daily round, the absence of dramatic events, especially the undercurrent of the maturation of the group of the people of God, who gradually solidify and learn to be free, and finally, the pressures of circumstances of inconvenience and difficulty. Temptation can have a positive outcome. In that case it will yield a consolidation of previous values as fruit of the sudden test. Thus, for example, the first book of Maccabees stresses that Abraham himself was tempted, and found faithful (1 Macc. 2:52; cf. Sir. 27:5, 7). Given human weakness, however, temptation can issue negatively, as well: if the pressure of the test exceeds the capacity to withstand it on human beings' part, temptation becomes the irreversible occasion of an erroneous choice (cf. Matt. 26:41; Mark 14:38; Luke 22:40, 46). Now the temptation, the trial, is added to the mystery of evil with which the human being is ever in contact. The mystery of evil means the mystery of inconsistent human weakness, as well. Thus an intervention from God as Father is sought in the form of a defense: that our entry upon the quicksands of those temptations whose result would be negative be prevented.

The experience of the people of God in the wilderness suggests another possible interpretation, one more consonant with the terminology used. Temptation, in Greek, which has an active meaning, rather than that of a temptation undergone, would indicate the temptation of which the human being becomes the protagonist. More than once, in the circumstances of the experience in the wilderness, the people are led to "tempt" God, to put God to the test (see Exod. 17:27; Deut 6:16; 9:22; Ps. 94:8). It is a negative attitude, contrasting with a trusting, unreserved abandonment that deserves God's care of the chosen people. But it is especially a lack in the character of filiation: it denotes a lack of trust, the seeking of a guarantee that would tranquilize the human being simply on the human level.

If temptation itself places us in contact with the mystery of evil, there is an intensification and an explicitation when evil is personified in the "evil one": the demonic element, Satan. The experience that Christians may have had, whether in personal experience or in a familiarity with the Old Testament, indicates a complex network of dangers, negativities, that, concretizing in their history, tend to engulf them. Christians know that they have weak points, of which the demonic element could take advantage, and it is difficult even to take account of them all. This situation — which could issue in drastic tension — ought not to impact upon the basic serenity of the children of God. God as Father has defeated evil in history from the beginning, vanquishing it through the death of Christ. God can then defend these children adequately, not only by putting them on their guard, but by actually snatching them from the grasp of the "evil one."

At bottom, this last petition constitutes a reference to Christians' precarious situation. They must not deceive themselves. They must not believe, even though they are indeed children of God, that they have arrived at a level of security that would put them out of all danger: in actual fact, we are always en route. And so they beseech the Father to watch over their path, to deliver them even from themselves, from those zones of attack of the "evil one" of which they feel themselves to be, and are, the vessels.

Finally, let us note — understanding "temptation" either in the sense of test to the limit, or in the active sense — that the Our Father entrusts to God our fears as well as the danger of doing evil and, finally, of failing in confidence in God. The emphasis is not laid on a voluntarism that would stimulate the human being, but rather God is asked to grant even what ought to come from the human being. Conscious that they are weak and fragile, capable of falling short even in their basic undertakings, instructed as they are to this effect by the mystery of evil, Christians entrust to God even these negative eventualities. They are not caught in their own short circuit, but bravely cast themselves into their Father's arms.

The Our Father, Synthesis of the Gospel

Having analyzed the formulation of the Our Father in Matthew, we wonder whether we might be able to find, still in the orbit of Matthew, echoes of the thematics emerging from the individual petitions. The response is surprisingly positive: the echoes and the developments are manifold. Let us select some examples.

First, let us consider the expression "Our Father, who art in heaven," which recalls the expression "heavenly Father." As we have stressed, the term "heavenly" as used of God, and explicitly of God as Father, is typical of Matthew. Of the seven

occurrences of "heavenly" referring to the Father, two are to
God as Jesus' Father ("my heavenly Father," Matt. 15:13;
18:45), while five are uttered by Jesus with reference to Christians ("your heavenly Father," Matt. 5:48; 6:14, 26, 32; cf.
23:9). When Christians receive Jesus' message, and precisely
to the extent that they do so, something passes from Jesus
to them. And once "my heavenly Father" has become "your
heavenly Father," Christians will be in a position to say, "Our
Father, who art in heaven."

We find, then, a development (if only implicit) of the concept of a sharing in God's "holiness," expressed in the petition
for the hallowing of the divine "name." When Jesus insists that
persons have the same attitudes as their heavenly Father, then
that they be able to love as God loves, forgive as God forgives,
act as God acts, in conformity with what God is, he is ap-
pealing to the transcendent reality proper to God — to God's
holiness. It is possible, for example, to employ the goodness
employed by the heavenly Father, since, as children who assimilate God from within, we share God's holiness in its roots
(cf. Matt. 5:48).

As for the petition for the coming of the Reign, we find a
more ample development in Matthew than in the other evan-
gelists. The Reign of God — which Matthew calls "kingdom of
heaven" thirty-three times, and twice the "kingdom of the Father" (cf. Matt. 13:43; 26:29) — is embodied in the Church,
which is the situation that emerges when the gift of Christ
granted by the Father is received by human beings. From this
situation emerge the reality, the sequence in time, and the eschatological scope of the Reign of God. The "parables of the
Reign" (cf. Matt. 13:1–51; see 13:11) are characteristic: in
them the "kingdom of heaven," the Reign of the Father, is seen
in its becoming, with the characteristic development that we
have observed above.

The appeal that God's will be optimally realized is especially suggested by the context in which the formulation of the
Our Father is situated: the Sermon on the Mount. The Sermon

on the Mount contains an ample, detailed documentation of what is the will of God as Father — the Father's "ambitions," we might say — for the children of God. The petition for the full actualization of the will of God fully coincides with Jesus' insistence, altogether clear if merely implicit, that what is indicated in the Sermon on the Mount, from its introduction in the Beatitudes to the factual acceptance of the word of God with which it concludes, be grasped and executed. We find all of this reinforced and developed in the insistence, again typical of Matthew, on the will of the Father: here is a caring will, unwilling that any of the least ones be lost (Matt. 18:14), requiring a concrete actualization above and beyond empty words (Matt. 7:21), and producing the most intimate tie with Jesus (Matt. 12:50). It is Jesus himself who effects the maximal fulfillment of the will of the Father when, in Gethsemane, he prays, "Your will be done" (Matt. 26:42).

The petition for daily bread — in the broad sense that we have illustrated — finds a continuity and an explanation in Matthew when the urgency of a complete trust in God is underscored with regard to food and raiment, day by day, precisely in the daily: "Today's trouble is enough for today" (Matt. 6:34).

The petition for a remission of "debts" directly proportional to that practice by Christians toward their own "debtors" is found mirrored in the urgency of acceptance, forgiveness, and mercy, and is particularly emphasized by Matthew. The most involving passage is the parable of the two debtors (Matt. 18:21–35). The bounty of the master, who "out of pity" condones an immense debt, if grasped and appreciated adequately by the slave who owes the debt, ought to incline the slave to bounty and mercy in his own turn, on the horizontal level, where debts are immeasurably less weighty. Jesus' words are taxing: "So my heavenly Father will do to every one of you, if you do not forgive your brother or sister from your heart" (Matt. 18:35). Jesus requires an unconditional openness to the Father's goodness, but not a passive openness and acceptance.

The infinite bounty of the Father must be personalized — reinterpreted, and assimilated by the person who wishes to be truly a child of God.

The petition not to enter into temptation presents, in the episode of Jesus' temptations, a touchstone of the critical points upon which the pressure activated by the demonic element can strike. Jesus is "tempted" to turn to his own advantage his ability to work miracles. It is precisely a question of bread, the bread necessary for life. After his fast, Jesus feels the need of this bread, this aliment, but he entrusts himself completely to God. He is truly the Son of God, but he will direct this qualification of his only to the service of others (cf. Matt. 4:2–4). Many temptations take advantage of the need for daily bread, revolving about the need the human being has for the nutrients, the indispensable elements — at least they believe them such — for their life. Persons must toil, they must be assiduous, but most of all they must keep in mind the exigency to "strive first for the kingdom of God and his righteousness," since all the rest "will be given to you as well" (Matt. 6:33). The Christian need only ask.

Another area where temptation strikes is confidence in God. The evil one's suggestion to Jesus is symptomatic: by a word, Jesus could commit God to something, could force God to do something in his behalf (Matt. 4:5–6). This kind of temptation occurs by way of a concoction of calculations by which human beings are inclined to close off what belongs to God — God's existence, word, interventions, providence — in the vicious circle of their own reasoning. "If there were a God, this would not be happening." It is a dangerous temptation, from which one is delivered only through the renewal of unconditional trust in God, whose ways are not our ways. The human being must not "put God to the test" (cf. Matt. 4:7). This is the demand of the Our Father in one of the two interpretations proposed.

The third area is more evident. Jesus is proposed an earthly reign. Here is the temptation of an absolute evaluation, in a vicious circle, of the contingent, sensible, and material. Generally speaking, this temptation will be inevitable. It may even be useful. Maintaining themselves — like Jesus — in a situation of dialogue with the heavenly Father, and speaking to God about their temptations, as well, Christians will avoid this risk of isolation, of readily interrupted contact, into which the disciples fell in Gethsemane, despite Jesus' warning.

Deliverance from the "evil one" — the last petition presented to the Father — acquires typical relief in the Gospel of Matthew, who uses the term with characteristic frequency. The rather broad spectrum of attributions presents a unitary articulation: there is a root of evil constituted by the demonic element (Matt. 5:37; 13:19), which tends to germinate in the hearts of persons who accept its pressure and who are consequently called "children of the evil one" (Matt. 13:38). Having become active protagonists of evil (Matt. 9:4), they "utter all kinds of evil" (Matt. 5:11). The murky wave of evil will threaten to engulf Christians, too, and they must defend themselves against it with determination (cf. Matt. 6:23; 13:19). In a word, there is a whole organized network of "evil" — the opposite of God's goodness (cf. Matt. 20:15) — issuing from the demonic element and tending to ensnare the human being. Only contact with the Father, which renders Christians children of God and homogeneous to God, can keep them safe and sound.

We could go on with the echoes of the Our Father in this Gospel. Those that we have seen are adequate to make an important fact almost palpable. The Our Father branches out until it has penetrated nearly everywhere in the Gospel of Matthew. Besides being synthesized in a schema, and perhaps already being recited in the liturgy, the "formula" broadly permeated the polyvalent life of the Matthean community.

At this point we more readily understand the Our Father as the "synthesis of the Gospel." With this prayer, every believer invokes the Father's mercy, knowing that this Father is the true, genuine face that Jesus has revealed. In sum, with the Our Father, all discover, ever more profoundly, who they are and to what they have been called. On the strength of the revelation of the visage of God as Father, Jesus teaches all human beings to recompose within themselves the same divine figure of parenthood. This means: love that forgives, attention to every need, comfort and assistance in everything — in short, God's constant nearness, which bestows on each of us the true new life that knows no end.

> How great is the indulgence of the Lord, how great the abundance of His regard for us and His goodness, that He has thus wished us to celebrate prayer in the sight of God, so as to call the Lord "Father" and, as Christ is the son of God, ourselves also so to be pronounced the sons of God, which name no one of us would dare to take in prayer, had not He Himself permitted us so to pray. So, most beloved brethren, we ought to remember and to know that, when we speak of God, we ought to act as sons of God, so that, just as we are pleased with God as Father, so too He may be pleased with us. Let us live as if temples of God, that it may be clear that the Lord dwells in us. Let not our acts depart from the Spirit, that we who have begun to be spiritual and heavenly may ponder and do nothing except the spiritual and the heavenly, since the Lord God Himself has said: "Those who glorify me, I shall glorify; but they that despise me, shall be despised" (cf. 2 Kings 2:30). The blessed Apostle also in his Epistle has laid down: "You are not your own, for you have been bought at a great price. Glorify God and bear him in your body" (1 Cor. 6:19, 20).[5]

---

5. Saint Cyprian, *De Dominica Oratione*, no. 11. Eng. trans.: Saint Cyprian, "The Lord's Prayer," in *Treatises,* trans. and ed. Roy J. Deferrari, The Fathers of the Church: A New Translation 36 (New York: Fathers of the Church, 1958), 135–36.